PROFITABLE PIG FARMING MADE EASY IN WEST AFRICA

YEMI ADESINA

Disclaimer

Every reasonable effort was made to ensure that the material in this book is accurate, correct, complete, and appropriate in writing. Nevertheless, the publishers and the author do not accept responsibility for any omission or error or any injury, damage, loss or financial consequences arising from the use of this book. Views expressed in the articles are those of the author and not the Editor or Publisher.

APOLOGIA

There are bound to be – only a few, I hope – errors and omissions, and I apologise in advance. No man knows it all, especially me! And you learn more as you get older. One good thing that comes with age is that you are happy to confess what you don't know and pass the inquiry on to a specialist who probably does.

This book is dedicated to hardworking, patient, enthusiastic, generally under-rewarded, and underappreciated people of Africa, those at home and in the diaspora, and everyone interested in the welfare of the continent of Africa.

CONTENTS

ACKNOWLEDGMENTS

Although one man has written this book, it wouldn't have been possible without the many people who have been so inspirational and whose research and hard work were helpful during its writing.

I thank God Almighty for His grace to research and put my findings into a book.

I also owe much to the many people who have encouraged me to follow my dream. In particular, my late dad, Mr Solomon Olajide Adesina. And to Bola, my wife of 27 years of marriage. I thank her immensely for her undying love, support, and encouragement, which allowed me to travel, research, and practise farming in Africa for many years.

For my two sons, Femi and Seun, whose input as the second-generation African diaspora in the United Kingdom makes the book more relevant to younger Africans. I want to thank them for our lengthy chats and the healthy debates that lasted late into the night and early mornings to gather their perspectives on specific topics. Their generation and those following beyond will move Africa further into the future.

I also extend my gratitude to the countless individuals, scholars, experts, and ordinary citizens who have contributed to the body of knowledge that informs these pages. The voices of Africa are vast and varied, and it is our privilege to have been able to amplify some of them. We encourage readers to delve deeper, seek more perspectives, and engage in the ongoing discourse shaping Africa's narrative.

THE AUTHOR

Mr Yemi Adesina is not your average author; he is a visionary on a mission to transform Africa. With a rich blend of expertise in social work, farming, and African history, Mr Yemi is a multifaceted leader dedicated to driving positive change across the continent.

As the CEO of Pristine Integrated Farm Resources Ltd, a non-profit organization, Mr Yemi is committed to promoting youth and rural empowerment, alleviating poverty through education, and elevating subsistence farming to thriving commercial enterprises in Africa. His passion for sustainable agriculture is evident in his comprehensive guide, "Profitable Pig Farming: A Step-by-Step Guide to Commercial Pig Farming from an African Perspective," which offers valuable insights into the agricultural landscape.

Not only does Mr Yemi excel as a farmer and advocate for rural development, but he is also a prolific trainer. His YouTube channel, "papayemo1," boasts a collection of 150 videos covering farming techniques and African history. With over 2.5 million viewers from more than 36 countries, his channel is a testament to his dedication to sharing knowledge and empowering individuals across the globe.

Mr. Yemi's written works are a testament to his deep understanding of Africa's challenges and potential. From "Why Africa Cannot Feed Itself and the Way Forward" to "Does the World

Need Africa," his books tackle critical issues facing the continent with a forward-thinking perspective.

Having emigrated to the United Kingdom in 1991, Mr. Yemi pursued two master's degrees, one in business administration and another in social work. After two decades of academic and professional growth, he made the life-changing decision to return to Nigeria in 2010. His goal was clear: contributing significantly to Africa's food production and driving positive change in his homeland.

In essence, Mr Yemi Adesina embodies the spirit of diaspora return, armed with expertise, passion, and an unwavering commitment to Africa's progress. His journey from the United Kingdom to Nigeria is a testament to his dedication to making a meaningful impact.

Through his diverse experiences, comprehensive knowledge, and boundless enthusiasm, Mr. Yemi Adesina is not just an author but a catalyst for change. His work bridges the worlds of agriculture, history, and social progress, offering a beacon of hope and inspiration for the continent he calls home.

FOREWORD

Pig farming has long been a vital part of agriculture in West Africa, deeply rooted in the traditions and cultures of our communities. It not only provides a valuable source of high-quality protein but also serves as a sustainable means of income generation for countless families. As the demand for pork and related products continues to rise, the importance of pig farming cannot be overstated.

In this comprehensive guide, "Pig Farming Made Easy in West Africa," we embark on a journey to explore the intricacies of successful swine production in our region. West Africa's unique climate, culture, and agricultural landscape present challenges and opportunities for pig farmers. Through the pages of this book, we aim to equip you with the knowledge, skills, and resources needed to thrive in this dynamic industry.

This guide is not just a manual; it is a testament to the resilience and dedication of West African farmers. It encapsulates the collective wisdom of generations of men and women who have tended to their herds, cared for their pigs, and worked tirelessly to ensure their communities have access to nutritious food and sustainable livelihoods.

In the following chapters, you will find a wealth of information on various aspects of pig farming, from selecting the right breeds and managing pig health to optimizing growth and embracing sustainable practices. We have also delved into the crucial topics of marketing, financial management, and the future of pig farming in our region.

We hope this guide serves as a valuable resource for novice and experienced pig farmers, enabling you to overcome challenges, seize opportunities, and succeed in your endeavours. Pig farming is not merely a means of income but a pathway to food security, rural development, and a brighter future for West Africa.

We want to extend our heartfelt gratitude to the countless individuals, organizations, and experts who have contributed their knowledge and insights to this project. Their dedication to advancing pig farming in West Africa is genuinely commendable.

As you embark on your pig farming journey, remember that every pig you raise is not just a source of sustenance and income; it represents the resilience and determination of West African farmers. May your efforts be rewarded with healthy herds, bountiful harvests, and prosperous communities.

Together, we can ensure that pig farming in West Africa thrives, benefiting our families, communities, and region.

CHAPTER 1
INTRODUCTION

PIG FARMING, often called swine production, has a rich and enduring history in West Africa. It has been an integral part of our agricultural heritage for generations, providing a vital source of sustenance and livelihood for countless families across the region. As we stand at the threshold of a new era of African growth and development, pig farming is poised to play an even more significant role in West Africa's journey toward food security, economic prosperity, and sustainable agriculture.

Welcome to "Pig Farming Made Easy in West Africa," This book is designed to be your comprehensive companion on your journey to becoming a successful pig farmer in Africa. Whether you're a novice looking to start your first pig farm or an experienced farmer aiming to improve your existing operation, this guide offers valuable insights, strategies, and practical advice tailored to Africa's unique challenges and opportunities.

In "Pig Farming Made Easy in West Africa," we explore this dynamic and promising industry comprehensively. We recognize that pig farming is not without its challenges, but it is our firm belief that with the right knowledge, resources, and commitment, these challenges can be transformed into opportunities for growth and development.

Pig farming is a promising sector in African agriculture due to the increasing demand for pork and the suitability of pig farming to various climates and scales of operation. However, success in pig farming requires more than just a love for animals; it demands knowledge, planning, dedication, and a deep understanding of the local context.

This book will delve into every aspect of profitable pig farming, from choosing the right pig breeds and setting up a suitable farm infrastructure to managing health, nutrition, and finances effectively. We'll also explore sustainable and environmentally friendly practices that benefit your farm and community.

Throughout the book, you'll find practical tips, case studies, and real-world examples from successful African pig farmers who have navigated the challenges and reaped the rewards of this industry. By the time you finish reading, you'll be equipped with the knowledge and confidence to embark on your profitable pig farming journey in Africa.

In this guide, we aim to demystify the art and science of pig farming, making it accessible to individuals of all backgrounds and levels of experience. Whether you are a novice looking to start your journey as a pig farmer or an experienced hand seeking to refine your techniques, this guide is designed to equip you with the knowledge and tools necessary for success.

The Structure of This Guide

This guide is divided into comprehensive chapters, each dedicated to a specific aspect of pig farming. From selecting suitable pig breeds to understanding pig behaviour, from managing pig health to marketing your products effectively, we cover the entire spectrum of swine production. Along the way, we provide practical tips, real-world insights, and actionable advice to help you navigate the challenges and seize the opportunities that pig farming offers in West Africa.

As you delve into the following chapters, you will discover a wealth of information, strategies, and best practices that reflect the unique characteristics of our region. We emphasize sustainable and eco-friendly farming methods, the importance of biosecurity, and the role of pig farming in rural development and food security.

Ultimately, this guide is a testament to the resilience and determination of West African pig farmers. It is a celebration of our shared heritage and a vision for a brighter future, where pig farming is not just a source of sustenance and income but a catalyst for positive change in our communities.

We thank the experts, farmers, and organizations contributing their expertise and insights to this project. Together, we can unlock the full potential of pig farming in West Africa, ensuring a prosperous and sustainable future for generations.

Now, let's begin this enriching journey into the world of profitable pig farming, where innovation, dedication, and a commitment to excellence are the keys to success.

The title " Profitable Pig Farming Made Easy in West Africa," " was chosen for several specific reasons:

1. **Clarity**: The title communicates the book's main focus, which is pig farming, with a specific emphasis on profitability and a perspective tailored to the African context. This clarity helps potential readers immediately understand what the book is about.
2. **Relevance**: Pig farming is a significant and growing industry in Africa due to the increasing demand for pork, making it a relevant and timely topic for those in the region interested in agriculture and entrepreneurship.

3. **Aspiration**: The word "Profitable" in the title emphasizes the book's goal to help readers start pig farming and succeed and profit from it. Many individuals are interested in profitable ventures, and this title captures their attention.

4. **Step-by-Step Guide**: This phrase indicates that the book will provide a structured, easy-to-follow approach to pig farming, making it suitable for beginners and experienced farmers who want to improve their practices.

5. **Commercial Pig Farming**: The word "commercial" highlights that the book covers the business side of pig farming, including aspects like marketing, finances, and sustainability, which are crucial for those looking to turn their farm into a profitable business.

6. **African Perspective**: This part of the title emphasizes that the book is specifically tailored to the African context. African agriculture often faces unique challenges and opportunities, and African readers can expect guidance and insights directly applicable to their circumstances.

In summary, the title "Profitable Pig Farming: A Step-by-Step Guide to Commercial Pig Farming from an African Perspective" effectively encapsulates the book's content, target audience, and purpose, making it an enticing and informative choice for anyone interested in the subject matter.

CHAPTER 2
FOREWARNED FOR NEW PIG FARMERS

BEFORE YOU EMBARK on your pig farming journey, it's essential to heed some crucial advice. Consider these key points before committing your time and resources to pig farming:

1. **Commitment:** Pig farming is unlike other businesses; it's not easily stopped with the press of a button. Once you begin, it can be challenging, if not impossible, to halt operations. Start small, devote time, energy, and funds to the setup and management, and be prepared for the long haul. While you may employ staff and a manager, strive to understand the basics of your business. Learn and ask questions actively.

2. **Start Small:** Many new farmers aspire to reach large-scale commercial pig farming overnight. However, starting small within your manageable limits is crucial based on your budget, knowledge, experience, and training. Beginning small limits your capital exposure to potential failures and allows you to learn and grow gradually.

3. **Grow Organically:** Begin your farm with a minimum viable number of pigs, which you can use to achieve your initial milestones. This approach focuses your energy and

resources on starting with a small number of breeder pigs and growing your herd from within.

4. **Be Market-Oriented:** Start attracting buyers and selling pigs as early as possible. Alongside breeder pigs, purchase additional weaners to fatten and sell within the first six months. This initial sale acts as a pilot test and helps spread the word about your farm within the pig-buying community.

5. **Manage Infrastructure Costs:** Avoid overinvestment in farm infrastructure, as it can delay operations and strain your initial budget. Focus on essential infrastructure for pig welfare and adhere to your budget.

6. **Maintain Good Hygiene:** Prioritize farm hygiene, as poor cleanliness can lead to reduced feed conversion and lower productivity. Regularly consult with veterinarians, maintain cleanliness, and ensure pigs' welfare.

7. **Focus on One Thing:** Resist the temptation to multitask with various farming ventures simultaneously. Concentrate on pig farming initially to become proficient before diversifying into other projects.

8. **Know Your Farm:** Cultivate the habit of systematically observing your pig farm weekly. This practice helps you understand pig behaviour, health, and growth stages, fostering a deeper connection with your animals and business.

By heeding these warnings and embracing these practices, you set the stage for a successful and fulfilling journey into the world of pig farming. Pig farming is not just a business; it's a responsibility to yourself, your animals, and your community

CHAPTER 3
TERMINOLOGIES

- Boar - mature, uncastrated male
- Sow - mature female after one or two pregnancies
- Gilt - young female swine before farrowing
- Farrow - giving birth to young ones
- Litters - young ones (piglets)
- Piglet - from when the baby pig is born and through the suckling period
- Weaners - when the suckling period is ended, and the piglets are removed from the sow, the piglets are called weaners
- Growers - Piglets are called weaners until they reach 20kg live weight. At this stage, they are called growers
- Business plan: Statement of business goals and the process to attain them.
- Marketing plan: Efforts to be taken to meet the sales target of a product.
- Six Ps of marketing: Price, product, people, place, promotion, policy.
- Variable costs: Inputs' costs that vary with production volume level. Examples include feed, fertilizer and seed.

- Fixed costs: Costs that remain unchanged irrespective of level of production or revenue. Examples include building rent and taxes.
- Working capital: Funds required for a short period in business, normally less than a year.
- Fixed capital: Funds required for financing long-term business assets, e.g. construction of a piggery unit or slaughterhouse.

CHAPTER 4
UNDERSTANDING THE POTENTIAL OF PIG FARMING IN WEST AFRICA

IN THE VAST tapestry of West African agriculture, pig farming stands out as a promising and economically viable endeavour. This section delves into the unique potential that pig farming holds within the West African context, shedding light on the factors that make it a compelling choice for farmers, entrepreneurs, and communities across the region.

The Rising Demand for Pork
Changing Diets and Urbanisation

West Africa is undergoing a dietary transformation driven by urbanisation, rising incomes, and changing consumer preferences. Pork, once a relatively uncommon meat in many West African diets, is gaining popularity. Understanding the factors behind this shift and the increasing demand for pork is crucial for aspiring pig farmers.

Market Opportunities and Profitability

Explore the potential profitability of pig farming by analysing market dynamics, pricing trends, and the economic feasibility of pork production in West Africa. Learn about the various market channels and opportunities for pig farmers to tap into this growing demand.

Economic Opportunities in Pig Farming

Job Creation and Livelihoods: Pig farming has the potential to generate employment and provide sustainable livelihoods, particularly in rural areas. Discover how the pig farming industry contributes to job creation and helps alleviate poverty.

Income Diversification: Explore how pig farming can serve as a source of income diversification for both smallholder farmers and larger agricultural enterprises. Understand the role of pig farming in reducing economic vulnerability.

Challenges and Solutions

Disease Management: Diseases pose a significant challenge to pig farming in West Africa. Learn about common pig diseases in the region, their prevention, and management strategies.

Feeding and Nutrition: Discover the intricacies of pig nutrition and feeding practices in West Africa. Explore cost-effective feeding strategies and the utilisation of local feed resources.

Infrastructure and Investment: Identify the infrastructure and investment requirements for successful pig farming operations in West Africa. Consider solutions to overcome barriers to entry.

Regulatory and Cultural Factors: Navigate the regulatory landscape for pig farming in West Africa, and understand the cultural and social factors that may impact your business.

WHY PIG FARMING IN WEST AFRICA

The importance of pig farming in West Africa cannot be overstated. Pigs provide a versatile source of protein in the form of lean meat, contributing to improved nutrition and food security in our communities.

By the end of this section, you will have gained a comprehensive understanding of the potential that pig farming holds in West Africa. You'll be equipped with valuable insights into the growing demand for pork, the economic opportunities it presents, and the challenges you may encounter on your pig farming journey in this region. This knowledge will serve as a solid foundation for the steps and strategies detailed in the subsequent chapters of this guide.

Pig farming in West Africa, while presenting its own set of challenges, can be made relatively easier compared to some other regions for several reasons:

1. **Climatic Suitability**: West Africa generally has a climate conducive to pig farming. Pigs are adaptable to various temperatures, and West Africa's tropical climate can provide a suitable environment for their growth.
2. **Abundance of Local Feed Resources**: West Africa has access to various local feed resources, including crops like cassava, maise, and millet, which can be used to formulate pig feed. This reduces the reliance on expensive imported feed and makes pig farming more cost-effective.
3. **Rising Demand for Pork**: There is a growing demand for pork in many West African countries due to urbanisation, population growth, and changing dietary preferences. This increasing demand provides a ready market for pig farmers.
4. **Local Pig Breeds**: Some local pig breeds in West Africa are well-suited to the region's conditions. These breeds often resist common local diseases and thrive in the local environment.
5. **Entrepreneurial Opportunities**: Pig farming offers entrepreneurial opportunities for individuals and communities in West Africa. It can be started on a small

scale and gradually expanded as experience and resources grow.

6. **Potential for Integration**: Pig farming can be integrated into other farming systems, such as crop farming or poultry, to create more sustainable and diversified agricultural practices.

7. **Government and NGO Support**: In many West African countries, there is support from governments and non-governmental organisations (NGOs) for agricultural development, including pig farming. This support can come from training, access to credit, and improved infrastructure.

8. **Community and Cultural Acceptance**: In some West African cultures, pigs have traditional significance and are accepted as a source of livelihood. This cultural acceptance can facilitate pig farming activities.

However, it's essential to note that challenges such as disease management, inadequate infrastructure, limited access to veterinary services, and regulatory issues can still make pig farming a complex endeavour in West Africa. To make pig farming truly easy and profitable in the region, farmers must receive proper training, adopt modern farming practices, and have access to support systems that address these challenges effectively.

THE FUTURE OF PIG FARMING IN WEST AFRICA

The future of pig farming in West Africa holds both challenges and opportunities. As the region continues to experience demographic shifts, economic development, and changes in consumer preferences, pig farming is poised to play a significant role in food security, economic growth, and sustainable agriculture. In this chapter, we will explore the key trends and prospects shaping the future of pig farming in West Africa.

Increasing Demand for Protein

Growing Population

- West Africa's population is expected to continue its rapid growth, leading to increased demand for protein sources, including pork.
- Pig farming can help meet this demand due to the relatively short production cycle and high feed conversion efficiency of pigs.

Urbanization

- Urbanization trends in the region are driving changes in dietary preferences, with a greater emphasis on meat consumption.
- Pig farming can benefit from proximity to urban markets and the ability to supply fresh pork products.

Improved Breeding and Genetics

- Continued efforts to improve pig breeds and genetics can enhance productivity and adaptability to local conditions.
- Access to improved breeding stock and the dissemination of best practices can lead to higher-quality pork products.

Sustainable Farming Practices

- Increasing environmental awareness and concerns about the impact of agriculture on ecosystems are likely to drive the adoption of sustainable pig farming practices.
- Practices such as agroforestry, organic farming, and waste management will gain prominence.

Certification and Traceability

- Consumer demand for ethically and sustainably raised pork products may lead to the development of certification programs and traceability systems in the region.
- Pig farmers who meet these standards can access premium markets.

Technology and Innovation

- The adoption of digital tools and precision agriculture techniques can enhance farm management, data analysis, and resource utilization.
- Remote monitoring and sensor technology can improve livestock health and productivity.

Processing and Value Addition

- Investment in modern processing facilities and value-added products can increase the profitability of pig farming.
- Developing packaged and processed pork products can cater to diverse consumer preferences.

Market Access and Export Potential

- West Africa has the potential to tap into regional and international pork markets, including those in neighbouring countries and the global African diaspora.
- Adherence to quality standards and sanitary regulations is crucial for export success.

Local Partnerships

Collaborations with local restaurants, retailers, and foodservice providers can expand market access for pig farmers.

Direct marketing initiatives and farm-to-table concepts can gain popularity.

CHALLENGES IN PIG FRAMING

Pig farming, like any agricultural endeavour, comes with its own set of challenges. Successful pig farmers must navigate these challenges to maintain a healthy and profitable operation. Here are some common challenges faced by pig farmers and throughout this book, we will endeavour to address each of these challenges

1. **Disease Outbreaks**: Disease outbreaks, such as African Swine Fever (ASF) can have devastating effects on pig herds and can lead to significant economic losses.
2. **Biosecurity**: Maintaining high biosecurity standards to prevent disease introduction and spread requires careful management and investment in infrastructure and protocols.
3. **Feed Costs**: The cost of pig feed can account for a significant portion of operating expenses. Fluctuations in feed prices and availability can impact profitability.
4. **Market Price Volatility**: Pig farmers are vulnerable to fluctuations in pork prices, which can be influenced by factors such as consumer demand, global trade, and disease outbreaks.
5. **Environmental Regulations**: Pig farms must comply with environmental regulations to manage waste and prevent pollution. Meeting these requirements can be challenging and costly.

6. **High Initial Investment**: Establishing a pig farming operation requires a substantial initial investment in infrastructure, housing, and equipment.
7. **Housing and Infrastructure**: Maintaining clean and well-ventilated housing facilities for pigs can be labour-intensive and may require ongoing maintenance and investment.
8. **Labour and Management**: Managing a pig farm effectively requires skilled labor and efficient management practices. Finding and retaining qualified staff can be a challenge.
9. **Market Access**: Accessing markets and securing profitable sales channels for pork products can be challenging, especially for small-scale pig farmers.
10. **Competition**: The pig farming industry can be competitive, with larger operations often benefiting from economies of scale.
11. **Disease Resistance and Genetics**: Selecting and breeding disease-resistant and high-performing pig genetics can be complex and requires a good understanding of genetics.
12. **Regulatory Compliance**: Pig farmers must adhere to various regulations related to animal welfare, health, and food safety. Non-compliance can lead to fines and legal issues.
13. **Weather and Climate**: Weather conditions can affect pig farming operations. Extreme weather events can pose risks to pig health and infrastructure.
14. **Consumer Preferences**: Changing consumer preferences, such as a growing demand for organic or ethically raised pork, can impact production practices and market opportunities.
15. **Transportation and Logistics**: Ensuring the safe and efficient transportation of pigs to markets or processing facilities requires careful planning and adherence to transportation regulations.

Despite these challenges, many pig farmers have found success through effective management, continuous learning, and adaptation to changing circumstances. By addressing these challenges proactively and seeking support from industry organizations and agricultural experts, pig farmers can work towards building profitable and sustainable operations.

CHAPTER 5
A BRIEF HISTORY OF PIG PRODUCTION

PIG PRODUCTION, or pig farming, has a rich and ancient history that spans thousands of years and various cultures worldwide. Here is a brief overview of the history of pig production:

1. Domestication of Pigs (circa 5000-4000 BCE): The domestication of pigs is believed to have begun in multiple regions, including China, India, and parts of Europe and the Middle East. Early humans recognized the value of pigs as a source of food, leather, and other resources.

2. Ancient Cultures and Pig Farming (circa 3000 BCE - 1 CE): In many ancient civilizations, including those of Mesopotamia, Greece, and Rome, pig farming played a significant role. Pigs were raised for their meat, and their importance is evident in religious ceremonies and culinary traditions. The Romans, in particular, are known for their advanced pig farming practices.

3. Middle Ages and Feudalism (5th - 15th Century CE): During the Middle Ages in Europe, pig farming was a vital component of feudal agricultural systems. Pigs were often kept in forests to forage for food, making them a valuable source of meat for medieval communities.

4. Introduction of New Breeds (18th - 19th Century CE): The 18th and 19th centuries saw the development of new pig breeds in Europe, such as the Large Black, Gloucestershire Old Spot, and Berkshire. These breeds were often specialized for specific meat qualities and became popular among pig farmers.

5. Industrialization and Intensification (20th Century CE): The 20th century brought significant changes to pig farming with the advent of industrialization and the intensification of agriculture. Advances in genetics, nutrition, and veterinary science led to the development of highly productive pig breeds and the establishing of large-scale commercial pig farms.

6. Modern Pig Production (Late 20th Century - Present): Modern pig production facilities, characterized by controlled environments, advanced breeding programs, and scientific management practices, have become the norm in many parts of the world. This approach has allowed for increased efficiency in meat production.

7. Sustainable and Specialty Pig Farming (21st century): There has been a growing interest in sustainable and speciality pig farming in recent years. Consumers are increasingly seeking products from pigs raised in humane conditions and with an emphasis on animal welfare. This has led to the rise of organic, free-range, and pasture-based pig farming operations.

Today, pig production is a global industry that provides a significant portion of the world's meat supply. It has evolved from small-scale backyard operations to large commercial enterprises and continues adapting to changing consumer preferences, technological advancements, and environmental concerns. Pig farming remains a vital component of agriculture, contributing to food security and economic development in many countries worldwide.

UNDERSTANDING PIGS' BEHAVIOUR AND CHARACTER

Pigs, often referred to as the "intelligent scavengers" of the animal kingdom, possess complex behaviour patterns and distinct characteristics that farmers must comprehend to raise and manage these animals successfully. While pig farming offers tremendous economic potential, it also demands a nuanced understanding of pigs' behaviour and character to ensure their well-being and optimize production. This section will explore the key aspects of pigs' behaviour and character that farmers must know.

Social Creatures: Pigs are inherently social animals. They thrive in groups and form close bonds with their pen mates. Understanding their social nature is vital for housing and managing them effectively. Solitary confinement or isolation can lead to stress and behavioural problems.

Intelligence: Pigs are brilliant creatures, often compared to dogs regarding cognitive abilities. Their problem-solving skills, memory, and ability to learn commands make them highly trainable. Farmers can harness this intelligence for various purposes, from training for specific tasks to improving handling and management practices.

Exploratory Nature: Pigs are naturally curious and highly exploratory. They use their strong snouts to root and investigate their environment. This behaviour helps them forage for food in the wild. This behaviour can be harnessed in farming settings for efficient forage-based feeding systems.

Foraging Instinct: Pigs are natural foragers, and their behaviour reflects this instinct. They have a keen sense of smell and are skilled at locating food. Farmers should provide opportunities for pigs to engage in foraging behaviour, such as scatter-feeding or access to pasture, to stimulate their mental and physical well-being.

Aggression and Dominance: Like many social animals, pigs establish hierarchies within their groups. Understanding dominance behaviour and managing aggression among pigs is crucial to maintaining a harmonious group dynamic. Proper housing design and group management strategies can help minimize aggression.

Nest-Building Instinct: Female pigs, or sows, exhibit a robust nest-building instinct, especially when pregnant. They will gather materials and arrange them to create a comfortable nest for their piglets. Farmers should provide appropriate nesting materials and a quiet, secluded area for farrowing to facilitate this behaviour.

Communication: Pigs communicate through vocalizations, body language, and scent markings. Farmers who pay close attention to these cues can better understand the well-being and needs of their pigs. Distressed or sick pigs may exhibit altered behaviour or vocalizations, signalling a need for attention.

Routine-Oriented: Pigs are creatures of habit and thrive on routine. Farmers can use this trait by establishing consistent feeding and management schedules. Disruptions to routines can lead to stress and negatively impact pig health and behaviour.

Sensitivity to Environment: Pigs are sensitive to their environment, particularly temperature changes and climatic conditions. Proper shelter and climate control are essential to ensure their comfort and well-being.

Adaptability: Pigs are highly adaptable animals, capable of thriving in various environments and management systems. However, farmers should ensure that the chosen system aligns with their pigs' specific breed and age, as different breeds have varying needs and behaviours.

In conclusion, pigs' behaviour and character are multifaceted and intricate, reflecting their intelligence, social nature, and instinctual behaviours. Farmers who invest the time to understand and respect these aspects of pig behaviour are better equipped to provide for their pigs' welfare, enhance productivity, and ultimately succeed in pig farming. Recognizing and responding to pigs' behavioural cues can lead to a more harmonious and productive partnership between farmers and these remarkable animals.

THE KEY ATTITUDES OF A SUCCESSFUL COMMERCIAL PIG FARMER

Success in commercial pig farming is not solely determined by technical knowledge or financial resources; it is equally influenced by the attitudes and mindset of the farmer. A successful commercial pig farmer possesses a unique set of attitudes that drive decision-making, innovation, and resilience in the face of challenges. In this section, we will explore the key attitudes that underpin the success of commercial pig farming.

1. Passion and Dedication: At the heart of any successful commercial pig farmer is a deep passion for pigs and farming. This passion fuels dedication to the well-being of the animals and the business. A dedicated farmer is willing to put in the long hours and hard work required to ensure that pigs are raised in optimal conditions and that the farm operates efficiently.

2. Continuous Learning: Successful pig farmers are lifelong learners. They recognize the dynamic industry, with new technologies, research findings, and best practices emerging regularly. A commitment to staying informed and adapting to new information is crucial for maintaining a competitive edge.

3. Patience and Persistence: Like any agricultural endeavour, pig farming has its share of challenges and setbacks. Successful farmers approach these hurdles with patience and persistence. They understand that success is not immediate and that overcoming obstacles often takes time and tenacity.

4. Attention to Detail: Commercial pig farming demands meticulous attention to detail. Farmers must monitor every aspect of their operation, from pig health and nutrition to record-keeping and financial management. The ability to notice small changes or issues early on can prevent larger problems down the road.

5. Adaptability: Agriculture is inherently unpredictable due to factors like weather, disease outbreaks, and market fluctuations. Successful pig farmers are adaptable and flexible in their approach. They can adjust their strategies and make informed decisions even in the face of uncertainty.

6. Business Acumen: Pig farming is not just about raising animals; it's also about running a business. A successful farmer understands financial management, budgeting, and the economics of pig production. They make informed decisions that contribute to the profitability and sustainability of their operation.

7. Ethical and Sustainable Practices: Ethics and sustainability are at the forefront of modern agriculture. Successful pig farmers prioritize animal welfare, environmental stewardship, and community engagement. They recognize that these principles align with consumer expectations and contribute to long-term success.

8. Innovation and Risk-Taking: Commercial pig farming is not a static industry. Successful farmers are willing to embrace innovation and take calculated risks to improve their operations. Whether adopting new technologies, exploring alternative feed sources, or diversifying income streams, innovation drives success.

9. Communication and Networking: Building relationships with other farmers, industry experts, and stakeholders is essential. Successful pig farmers understand the value of networking and collaboration. These connections can provide access to valuable knowledge, support, and market opportunities.

10. Resilience and Problem-Solving: Adversity is a part of farming, and successful pig farmers possess resilience and practical problem-solving skills. When faced with challenges, they remain solution-oriented and maintain a positive outlook.

In conclusion, the attitudes of a successful commercial pig farmer extend beyond the pigpen. They encompass a passion for the industry, a commitment to learning, adaptability, business savvy, ethical principles, and a willingness to innovate and collaborate. These attitudes are the foundation upon which successful pig farming enterprises are built, ensuring profitability, sustainability, and long-term success in the ever-evolving world of commercial pig farming.

CHAPTER 6
STARTING YOUR OWN PIG FARM

STARTING your pig farm requires careful planning, knowledge, and a commitment to the well-being of the animals. Here's a step-by-step guide to help you get started:

1. Research and Education:

- **Learn About Pig Farming:** Begin by deeply understanding pig farming. Read books, attend workshops, take online courses, and seek advice from experienced pig farmers.
- **Choose Your Focus:** Decide the scale and type of pig farming you want to pursue. Options include breeding, raising piglets for sale, or producing pork for the market.

2. Business Plan:

- **Create a Business Plan:** Develop a comprehensive business plan that outlines your farm's goals, budget, financing needs, and expected return on investment. Include details about your target market and marketing strategies.

3. Location and Housing:

- **Select a Suitable Location:** Choose a location that provides good access to markets, transportation, and essential services. Ensure that zoning regulations permit pig farming in your chosen area.
- **Build Adequate Housing:** Construct clean, well-ventilated, and secure housing facilities for your pigs. Consider factors like temperature control, disease prevention, and space requirements based on the number of pigs you intend to raise.

4. Procure Equipment and Supplies:

- **Purchase Equipment:** Acquire equipment such as feeding troughs, waterers, and waste management systems.
- **Source Feed and Bedding:** Establish reliable suppliers for pig feed, bedding materials (e.g., straw or wood shavings), and veterinary supplies.

5. Obtain Breeding Stock:

- **Select Quality Breeding Stock:** Choose healthy and genetically superior breeding animals. Consider factors like breed, age, and lineage. Consult with experts or breed associations for guidance.
- **Breeding Program:** Develop a breeding program that outlines breeding schedules, mating pairs, and record-keeping for tracking breeding performance.

6. Animal Care and Nutrition:

- **Provide Proper Nutrition:** Develop a nutrition plan that meets the specific needs of your pigs based on their age, weight, and production stage. Work with a nutritionist if needed.

- **Health Management:** Implement a health management program that includes vaccinations, deworming, disease monitoring, and access to veterinary care.

7. Record-Keeping:

- **Maintain Detailed Records:** Keep accurate records of feed consumption, pig health, breeding, and financial transactions. Effective record-keeping is crucial for farm management and decision-making.

8. Marketing and Sales:

- **Identify Target Markets:** Determine your target markets, whether it's local consumers, restaurants, wholesalers, or niche markets like organic or heritage pork.
- **Marketing Strategies:** Develop marketing strategies to promote your products. Consider branding, online presence, farmers' markets, and partnerships with local businesses.

10. Start Small and Scale Gradually:

- **Begin Small:** It's advisable to start with a manageable number of pigs and scale up as you gain experience and confidence.

11. Continuous Learning:

- **Stay Informed:** Pig farming is a dynamic field. Stay informed about new technologies, best practices, and industry trends through ongoing education and networking with other farmers.

12. Seek Professional Advice:

- **Consult Experts:** Don't hesitate to seek advice from veterinarians, agricultural extension officers, or experienced pig farmers. They can provide valuable guidance and support.

13. Financial Management:

- **Manage Finances Wisely:** Keep a close eye on your farm's finances. Monitor expenses, income, and profitability regularly. Adjust your budget and business plan as needed.

Starting a pig farm requires dedication, hard work, and ongoing learning. It's essential to be prepared for challenges and setbacks along the way. You can establish a successful and sustainable pig farming venture with proper planning and a commitment to best practices in pig farming.

WHERE TO LOCATE YOUR PIG FARM

Choosing the right location for your pig farm is a critical decision that can significantly impact your farming venture's success. Like in real estate, the importance of location cannot be overstated in agriculture. The saying in real estate, "Location! Location!! Location!!!" is equally applicable to farming.

Acquiring the right piece of land for your farm is one of the most crucial steps you'll take as a farmer, and it's a decision that's challenging to reverse once you've made investments in construction and infrastructure. Many new farmers make the mistake of buying land without clearly understanding what they intend to produce, essentially putting the cart before the horse.

Ultimately, choosing where to locate your farm is personal, but several important factors should guide this selection process. This section provides vital information on the factors to consider when determining your farm's location.

1. **Proximity and Familiarity**: Ideally, your pig farm should be easily accessible from your workplace or residence, allowing you to visit regularly. Absentee farming can lead to various challenges, and regular visits help you stay informed about farm activities and address issues promptly. Your farm should be within a one to two-hour drive from your workplace or residence. Familiarity with the local culture and language is also advantageous, as it reduces reliance on interpreters and minimizes misunderstandings.

2. **Accessibility and Good Neighbourliness**: Ensure your farm has access to a well-maintained road, preferably close to the main road. Assess the route for potential issues during the rainy season, such as stream crossings that may flood. Good road access is essential for transporting supplies and pigs to the market. Selecting a location with a well-established market and few pig farms in the neighbourhood can be advantageous. Such areas often have readily available resources like feed, labour, and veterinary expertise.

3. **Size of Land**: The land size depends on your farming scale. A single acre can suffice for small-scale pig farms with around 1,000 pigs or more. However, starting small in your backyard with around 20 weaners is also possible, with plans to expand as your pig population grows. Ensure your choice of land allows for flexibility as your farming goals evolve. Access to 1 to 2 acres or more for a commercial pig farm provides space for waste management and expansion.

4. **Avoiding Medium or High-Density Areas**: Given the rapid urbanization in many African towns, it's wise to avoid purchasing farmland in medium to high-density areas too close to residential zones. Such areas can quickly urbanize, posing challenges as your pig farm expands. Pigs produce substantial waste, and a well-managed farm can experience rapid growth, resulting in increased waste production. Opting for 1 to 2 acres of farmland allows you to manage waste efficiently within your farm.

5. **Housing**: Proper housing, often called pig pens, is crucial for the well-being and productivity of your pigs. The housing should protect them from weather, diseases, and contamination. Adequate drainage is essential to ensure efficient waste management.

In summary, factors like proximity, accessibility, good neighbours, land size, and suitable housing should guide your decision when selecting the location for your pig farm."

When selecting the location for your pig pen, consider the following factors:

- Maintain a distance of at least 500 meters from residential areas to prevent odour and fly-related nuisances.
- Ensure convenient connectivity to good roads throughout the year, facilitating marketing efforts.
- Choose a location away from noisy and high-traffic areas to reduce stress for your pigs.
- Opt for an elevated, well-drained site to prevent flooding.
- Enable natural drainage and effluent disposal by constructing the pen on a slight slope.
- Prioritize ventilation, cleanliness, and exposure to sunlight.
- Ensure easy access to clean water sources, as pigs consume substantial water, and hygiene is crucial.

- Provide shade by planting large evergreen trees, such as plantain, banana, and papaya.
- Aim for a central location on the land to facilitate waste diversion and manure usage. j. Maintain open sides in your pig house for proper ventilation.

Orientation of the House: Ensure that the longest side of your pig pen, running from north to south, allows even sunlight distribution throughout the day. Adequate sunlight keeps the floor dry and minimizes disease risks.

Space: Pigs require ample room to move, eat, sleep, and defecate. Insufficient space can lead to fat accumulation rather than muscle growth, and it can also result in stress-related behaviours. Your pig cells should provide enough space for pigs to roam, eat, and rest comfortably, with separate areas designated for each activity.

By carefully considering these factors, you can choose the optimal location for your pig farm, setting the stage for a successful and efficient operation."

CONSTRUCTING A PIG FARM

Starting a successful pig farm requires careful planning, especially when it comes to choosing the right location, determining the size of your land, and designing suitable housing for your pigs. You need to focus on the construction of pens and creating environment that will allow the pigs to perform to their best .

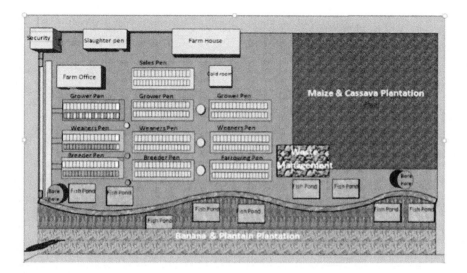

Breeder Pen

Once the land has been acquired, the foremost priority for the business is to construct enclosures and establish an environment conducive to optimal pig performance.

The breeding pen is the dedicated space where mature breeder pigs are housed upon arrival at the farm. These breeder pigs consist of mature male boars and mature female gilts, typically aged between 6 to 8 months. They play a pivotal role in the farm's reproductive cycle, as they are responsible for mating and birthing the piglets that will populate the farm. These valuable animals serve as the core production unit and typically remain on the farm for a period ranging from 3 to 5 years. Each breeder pig is housed in its enclosure.

The design of these enclosures is characterized by spaciousness and features a central corridor, facilitating easy movement for farm personnel. Importantly, this design ensures that staff can access each enclosure without traversing through another. This particular layout is most suitable for accommodating boars, gilts, and pregnant and nursing sows, essentially serving as a maternity pen.

The open design of these enclosures promotes unrestricted airflow, facilitating natural ventilation, providing ample space for each pig, and ensuring adequate illumination throughout the day. This design is essential for attendants to carry out proper management routines efficiently.

Note: To house 22 breeder pigs, you will require 24 of these individual enclosures. Additionally, allocate an extra two enclosures for sick and quarantine pigs.

Grower pen

As mentioned earlier in this report, a sow is pregnant for four months, and piglets born stay with the mum till they are weaned at 6 to 8 weeks old. The weaning process involves separating the piglets from the sow and placing all the piglets together into a group of 20 piglets in one room. This room will house the weaners till they reach either the market weight is called the grower pen.

For this project, we recommend that you build a minimum of 5 cells of 20 x 18 feet at a time to house 100 weaners to take advantage of the economy of scale when building.

The picture above is a typical six cells of 20 x 18 x 4 feet grower cell; the roof is tall to allow air movement in pen to cool the pen

Picture note in the picture, the height of the wall is one meter tall, and there are water nipples on the wall. Pigs love playing in the water to cool down, so you should consider building a water trough in each cell for them to play in and stay healthy. The water trough should be changed regularly and kept clean at all times. The door to each cell must be metal, allowing air to move through the pen. You should also make sure the drainage is kept clean and covered at all times to avoid insects, pests, diseases and contamination.

Office and Workers' Quarters

As the farm is located in a slightly remote place, you might need to build a farm house for staff with showers, a kitchen, a canteen, and a recreation room as well as bedrooms. This will not only reduce your staff absenteeism or turnover of staff and but also increase the security of your farm. A commercial farm should have offices where management stays while on the farm and where clerks kept production and financial records, received visitors, dispensed medicines and therapeutic drugs, and operated their computers.

A 3-bedroom farmhouse with 2 bathrooms and toilets and kitchen

OTHER CAPEX EXPENDITURE

These are other costs that a farmer needs to bear in mind. Some of them are optional, but from our experience, having them in your plan will make the management of your farm easier and cheaper in the long run.

Housing and Pens:

1. Invest in appropriate housing for your pigs.
2. Consider factors like ventilation, insulation, and space requirements.
3. Ensure pens are clean, secure, and designed to prevent injuries and escapes.

Water and Feeding Facilities: Install reliable water supply systems and feeding facilities. Pigs need access to clean water, and feeding equipment should allow for efficient feeding practices.

Waste Management: Implement a waste management system that complies with environmental regulations. This may involve proper disposal of pig waste or its use sustainably, such as composting.

Quarantine and Isolation Facilities: Designate an area for quarantine and isolation. This is crucial for disease control, as new pigs should be isolated before being introduced to the main herd.

Security Measures: Implement security measures to protect your pigs from theft or predation. Adequate fencing and surveillance can deter potential threats.

Record-Keeping Systems: Set up a comprehensive record-keeping system to track your pigs' health, growth, and performance. Accurate records are invaluable for making informed decisions.

Boreholes, Water tanks and Water nipples are mandatory on your farm

We will recommend that you start your farm with a functional farm infrastructure that uses affordable building material. As your farm expand and your staff gained more experience, you can automate and use more sophisticated material. You will need a good source of electricity.

CHAPTER 7
MEETING YOUR PIG'S NEEDS ON THE FARM

IN THIS CHAPTER, we delve into what your pigs require to not just survive but thrive on your farm. Understanding and meeting these needs are fundamental to the success of your pig farming venture. It's a symbiotic relationship where your goals as a farmer align with your pigs' needs. Let's explore what your pigs need:

Food: Providing quality and affordable feed is essential for your pigs. Here are key considerations:

- Determine the feed ingredients your pigs need.
- Assess local availability of feed ingredients.
- Decide whether to grow or purchase feed ingredients.
- Plan for land, funds, expertise, and labour if growing feed.
- Ensure that cultivating crops for feed doesn't distract from pig farming.
- Identify sources for purchasing feed ingredients.
- Consider transportation logistics and storage facilities.
- Decide between compounded concentrate or raw feed ingredients.
- Plan feed preparation methods.

- Establish feeding schedules and hygiene practices.

Water: Clean water is vital for your pigs' hydration and cooling. Consider these aspects:

- Explore local water sources and supply methods.
- Choose between municipal water, wells, or boreholes.
- Avoid using streams or rivers due to potential contamination.
- Plan for power sources for water pumping.
- Set up water storage solutions like tanks.
- Develop plumbing systems for water distribution.
- Select appropriate water containers (buckets, troughs, or nipples).
- Ensure regular cleaning of water containers.
- Implement cooling systems for hot weather.

Security: Protecting your pigs goes beyond theft prevention; it involves creating a safe environment. Consider these security measures:

- Prevent mixing of pigs unnecessarily.
- Avoid disturbances from external factors like passersby, buyers, or predators.
- Provide shelter from weather elements.
- Ensure dry floors and bedding for piglets.
- Implement biosecurity measures.
- Prevent the entry of pathogens from outside.
- Plan for regular pen cleaning.
- Consider netting to protect from insects.

Space: Adequate space is crucial for your pigs to perform various activities comfortably:

- Provide sufficient space for sleeping, eating, dunging, and foraging.
- Prevent aggression by allowing submissive pigs to escape.
- Plan dimensions for different categories of pig pens.

Air: Fresh air, good ventilation, and proper shelter are essential for your pigs:

- Ensure good airflow and ventilation in pig pens.
- Prevent drafts at lower levels while allowing air circulation.
- Keep pen walls at an optimal height.
- Use appropriate bedding materials.
- Address ammonia accumulation by improving drainage and waste removal.

Meeting these needs is pivotal for the well-being of your pigs and the profitability of your farm. As you progress through this book, you'll find answers to specific questions related to these needs based on your farm's location and circumstances.

CHAPTER 8
SUSTAINABLE PIG FARMING PRACTICES

SUSTAINABLE PIG FARMING represents a holistic approach to the swine industry, where the well-being of pigs, the environment, and farmers' livelihoods are harmonised. In an era of growing environmental concerns and an increasing global population, sustainable practices are essential to ensure the long-term viability of pig farming.

1. Environmental Stewardship

One of the core tenets of sustainable pig farming is environmental responsibility. Pigs, like all livestock, produce waste that can pose environmental challenges. Sustainable pig farms implement strategies to manage waste efficiently, reduce greenhouse gas emissions, and minimise their ecological footprint.

Manure Management: Sustainable farms use advanced manure management techniques, such as anaerobic digesters and composting, to convert pig waste into valuable resources like biogas and organic fertiliser.

Animal Welfare: Sustainable pig farming places a strong emphasis on the well-being of the animals. Happy, healthy pigs are not only ethical but also more productive.

- **Spacious Housing**: Providing pigs ample space to move, rest, and express natural behaviours improves their quality of life.
- **Enrichment**: Environmental enrichment, such as rooting materials and objects for play, helps combat boredom and stress.
- **Healthcare**: Regular veterinary care and health monitoring ensure that pigs are free from pain, disease, and distress.
- **Social Interaction**: Pigs are social animals; sustainable farms group pigs to promote social interactions and prevent loneliness.
- **Feed Efficiency**: Sustainable farms use feed efficiently to minimise waste and reduce the environmental impact of pig farming. Precision nutrition and balanced diets are key.

Water Conservation: Implementing water-saving technologies and practices helps conserve this precious resource.

Market Responsiveness: Sustainable pig farms often respond to consumer demand for ethically raised, locally sourced pork products, allowing for premium pricing.

Efficient Resource Use: Reducing waste and optimising resource use can lower production costs and increase profit margins.

Education: Engaging with the community through educational programs and farm tours raises awareness about sustainable farming practices.

INDIGENOUS MICROORGANISMS (IMO)

Sometimes, a farm may opt for a deep litter system within each pig cell. This environmentally conscious approach helps reduce pollution of nearby water bodies such as rivers or streams. It is particularly favoured in high-density areas, such as locations near residential zones, with limited space for efficient pig waste disposal.

In such scenarios, the concrete flooring of each cell is replaced with bedding materials like untreated wood from sawmills, palm leaves, sawdust, wood shavings, and charcoal. These materials are treated with Indigenous Microorganisms (IMO), which are cultured and activated using lactic acid bacteria derived from fermented fruit juice, brown sugar, and maize bran (some may opt for rice bran).

Overripe fruits like oranges, bananas, grapes, mangoes, watermelons, etc., along with brown sugar, are soaked in a water tank for two weeks, with the addition of maize or rice bran to serve as feed for the microorganisms.

The term 'Indigenous' signifies the use of locally sourced bacteria specific to the piggery's location, making this system particularly effective. The process begins by chopping the fruit into small pieces, placing them in a large container, and adding 1kg of fruit to 1kg of brown sugar. The container is sealed with a paper or cloth cover, allowing air to enter and exit, and is left to ferment for 8-10 days. Afterwards, the fruit juice is extracted by straining it through a sieve and collected in a jar.

To prepare the IMO for application, 2 spoons of the extracted juice are added to 10 litres of water in a watering can. This mixture is then poured onto the bedding surface of the pig's pen.

Construction for IMO involves the option of concreting the inside of each cell of the pen, although concrete flooring is recommended. An aerobic floor base is created by arranging waste logs from sawmills, approximately six feet long by 4-6 inches in diameter, in parallel fashion, to form a foundation."

To reduce expenses, cover the logs with a layer of palm leaves approximately one foot thick. Next, distribute charcoal evenly over the foliage, followed by a generous layer of wood shavings, also one foot deep. Afterwards, apply the Indigenous Microorganisms (IMO) onto the bed of wood shavings.

Please note that these Indigenous Microorganisms are aerobic, requiring oxygen to thrive. The moisture levels and composition of the bedding foster the growth of these microorganisms, allowing them to proliferate throughout the structure. As the dominant bacteria within this system, they establish a symbiotic relationship between the pigs and themselves. They efficiently digest and decompose the pig's waste, including faeces and urine, without producing any unpleasant odours (due to their aerobic nature), thus creating a pleasant environment for the pigs.

If you ever detect any unpleasant odours emanating from the pen, it indicates that anaerobic bacteria are attempting to take control. In such cases, simply apply more IMO to bolster the population of aerobic bacteria and restore the balance."

BIOSECURITY FOR PIG FARMS: PROTECTING YOUR LIVESTOCK

Biosecurity encompasses the essential measures taken to safeguard a farm, its livestock, and its workforce from diseases. These measures serve a dual purpose: to prevent pathogens from entering the farm (external biosecurity) and to hinder the spread of disease within and to other farms if pathogens are already present (internal biosecurity).

In this section, we will focus on cost-effective and practical biosecurity measures that pig farmers can implement to deter infectious diseases from taking hold on their farms and eliminate existing pathogens to the extent possible. It's important to note that achieving absolute sterility on a farm is neither feasible nor desirable. Instead, the goal is to reduce pathogen levels to a point where the pig's natural defence mechanisms can manage any remaining pathogens effectively.

The Cost of Poor Hygiene

While pig farmers frequently discuss biosecurity, understanding the financial implications of subpar hygiene can motivate us to prioritize cleanliness. For entrepreneurial farmers driven by business sense, the financial losses resulting from poor hygiene should be a wake-up call.

Research conducted on UK pig farms revealed that poor hygiene can reduce food conversion in pigs by up to 30%. To put this in perspective, consider that for every 3 kg of daily feed costing, 30% is wasted as pigs use the feed to combat pathogens acquired due to poor hygiene. This is particularly concerning as feed costs account for 60-70% of total expenses, and feed prices have risen.

Poor hygiene also impacts sow and gilt productivity, leading to two fewer piglets per sow per litter. For instance, if a sow typically gives birth to 9 litters a year, poor hygiene results in losing four piglets annually.

Notably, subclinical diseases—low-level, invisible illnesses—can potentially cost farmers more over two years than a major outbreak.

Protecting Your Farm

Segregation is the foundational step in biosecurity. It involves keeping potentially infected or sick animals and materials away from uninfected ones. This practice aligns with the Yoruba adage, "If the wall is not cracked, a lizard cannot enter the house through the crack." Preventing pathogens from entering the farm is the most effective way to avoid infections. Control the entry of pigs from external farms, implement quarantine for newly acquired animals, limit sources of your animals, fence the farm area, and control access for people, birds, rodents, and especially pig buyers.

Cleaning is a fundamental and affordable biosecurity measure. All materials and vehicles entering or leaving the farm should be thoroughly cleaned to remove visible dirt, which also removes a majority of pathogens. Avoid borrowing farm equipment from other farms. Daily scraping, washing, and using detergent to clean pig pen floors and walls are crucial, as most pathogen contamination resides in dried-on excreta, faeces, and feed. Cleaning with soap helps eliminate these contaminants.

Disinfection should follow thorough cleaning. Disinfectants are applied to destroy infectious agents. It is essential to understand that disinfectants are only effective when cleaning is performed correctly and consistently. They should be the final step in biosecurity and work best after comprehensive cleaning. Contrary to common assumptions, disinfectants won't penetrate dirt effectively or be present long enough to kill bacteria if floors or walls aren't thoroughly cleaned. Additionally, organic materials can inactivate disinfectant power. Thus, cleaning is as vital, if not more so, than disinfection.

After cleaning and disinfecting, materials and vehicles should be allowed to dry before reuse. Observe a minimum 3-day downtime for proper drying to re-populate pig pens with new pigs.

Other Good Practices:

- Ensure new pigs introduced are disease-free.
- Implement quarantine for newly purchased pigs.
- Encourage age-segregated rearing and avoid co-mingling pigs of different health statuses.
- Adopt an all-in-all-out management system.
- Promote proper fencing and measures to control contact with birds, rodents, cats, and dogs.
- Develop farm protocols for visitors and enforce hygiene measures.
- Assign farm-specific instruments or equipment for use on the farm.

- Regularly clean the pig unit, including daily removal of manure.
- Thoroughly clean pens before disinfection.
- Plan the physical location of herds to maintain adequate distances from neighbouring farms.
- Invest in staff training and education in disease control.
- Prioritize the control of feedstuffs, water, wildlife, and human visitors.
- Apply strict biosecurity measures at slaughterhouses, focusing on bio-containment.

Pigs are susceptible to various diseases that can impact productivity and profits. Implementing comprehensive biosecurity practices is essential for safeguarding your pig farm and ensuring the health and well-being of your livestock.

CHAPTER 9
CHOOSING THE RIGHT PIG BREEDS

WHEN EMBARKING on your pig farming venture, the initial step is to select healthy pigs carefully. The choice of pig breeds will largely depend on your intended market and the desired farm output. Commencing your pig farm with subpar breeds is a detrimental mistake that can significantly impact your farm's profitability. The quality of your chosen breed, the quality of feed provided, and the adequacy of housing all play pivotal roles in determining your farm's ability to meet its goals.

Choosing the Best Breed

As a farmer and educator, I am frequently asked which pig breed is best for a farm. My response is that the choice depends on the specific goals of your farm, a response that may only sometimes align with people's expectations. Many anticipate a recommendation for an exotic breed that has been imported into Africa.

However, as a pig farmer and an educator, I consistently emphasize the importance of "profitability" during my training sessions. This is because I have observed numerous farmers who launched their farms with high-performing exotic pig breeds recently introduced to Africa needing to grasp the fundamental principles of pig farming fully. These imported pigs and their associated feed (concentrate) are prohibitively expensive. Given the current pig market dynamics and pork prices in West Africa, such farmers often need help to break even despite their commendable efforts, expertise, and substantial capital investments.

In contrast, I have found that hybrid pigs (crossbreeds between an exotic breed and a locally popular breed), while performing slightly below high-performing exotic breeds, are more profitable when considering return on investment in fixed and working capital. The key consideration when selecting the right breed for your farm should revolve around several factors:

1. Addressing and correcting any deficiencies in your existing pig population.
2. Suitability for your target market.
3. Improvement in the profit margin of your production costs.
4. A proven track record of performance.
5. Adaptability to your climate and farm environment.

In sub-Saharan Africa, pig breeds generally fall into four categories:

Indigenous or Local Types: These pigs are hardy, with stunted growth and poor reproductive performance. They exhibit various skin colours, pointed snouts, and sharp feet. They are adapted to local feed and water conditions but are becoming rarer due to hunting and past African Swine Fever outbreaks.

Popular Breeds: These pigs are crossbreeds from local and exotic breeds, like Large White, Landrace, and Hampshire. They are popular among small-scale farmers for their perceived fast growth and better returns.

Exotic Breeds: Exotic breeds like Duroc, Landrace, and Yorkshire offer high yields but come with a higher cost and may not thrive under tropical conditions.

Crossbreeds (Hybrids): Crossbreeding combines different breeds, resulting in hybrid vigour and improved traits. Hybrids are well-suited to local conditions and have advantages like lower rearing costs and disease resistance.

Selecting the right breed is crucial for a successful pig farming operation, considering factors like growth rates, feed efficiency, and environmental adaptability."

Native West African Breeds

The West African Dwarf Pig

Native to West Africa, this small-sized breed is adapted to the region's tropical climate. They are known for their hardiness, resistance to common local diseases, and suitability for small-scale farming systems. West African Dwarf Pigs are ideal for smallholder farmers looking to start pig farming.

The Nigerian Pig

Another native breed to West Africa, Nigerian Pigs are slightly larger than the West African Dwarf Pigs. They are appreciated for their meat quality and adaptability to local conditions. These pigs are known for their reproductive efficiency, making them a popular choice for breeding purposes.

Exotic Breeds

Large White (Yorkshire): The Large White breed is renowned for its prolificacy and lean meat production. They are known for their excellent growth rate, making them a top choice for commercial pig farming. However, they may require careful management in hot and humid climates.

Landrace: Landrace pigs are highly adaptable and thrive in various climates. They are known for their exceptional mothering abilities and large litters. Landrace pigs are valued for their lean meat and can be a suitable choice for intensive pig farming operations.

Duroc: Duroc pigs are prized for their meat quality, especially their marbling and flavor. They have a good feed conversion rate and adapt well to different environments. Duroc is often used in crossbreeding programs to improve meat quality in commercial operations.

Hampshire: Hampshire pigs are recognized for their muscular build and rapid growth. They are known for their high-quality meat, with good marbling and flavor. Hampshire pigs are suitable for both intensive and outdoor farming systems.

Crossbreeding Strategies

Hybrid Vigor: Many commercial pig farmers opt for cross-breeding programs to leverage the strengths of different breeds. Crossbred pigs often exhibit hybrid vigor or heterosis, which results in improved growth rates and disease resistance. Popular crossbreeds include Large White x Landrace and Duroc x Hampshire.

Specific Goals: When implementing crossbreeding, it's essential to have clear objectives. Some farmers prioritize meat quality, while others focus on reproductive efficiency or adaptability to local conditions. Tailor your crossbreeding strategy to meet your specific goals.

Breeding Programs: Seek guidance from experienced breeders when developing a crossbreeding program. Proper record-keeping and breeding stock selection are critical for your program's success.

Production Goals: Determine your production goals, whether it's lean meat production, high reproductive rates, or a balance between the two. Your goals will influence the choice of breeds and breeding strategies.

Market Demand: Research market demand and consumer preferences for pork in your region. Select breeds that align with market demands to maximize profitability.

COMMON PIG DISEASES IN WEST AFRICA

Pigs can be susceptible to various diseases, some of which can have significant economic and health implications for pig farmers. Here are some common pig diseases:

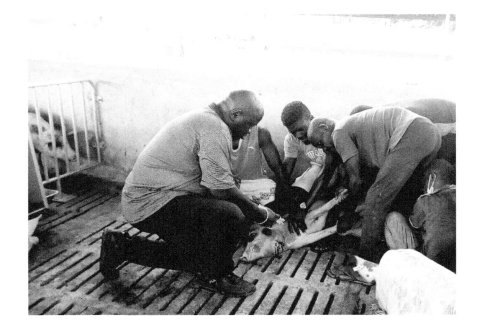

African Swine Fever (ASF):

- ASF is a highly contagious and deadly viral disease that affects domestic and wild pigs.
- It can spread rapidly and has a high mortality rate.
- There is no vaccine or cure for ASF, so prevention through biosecurity measures is crucial.

Foot-and-Mouth Disease (FMD):

- FMD is a highly contagious viral disease that affects cloven-hoofed animals, including pigs.
- It causes fever, blister-like sores on the mouth, tongue, and hooves, and can lead to significant economic losses due to reduced meat and milk production.
- Vaccination is used in some regions to control FMD.

Porcine Reproductive and Respiratory Syndrome (PRRS):

- PRRS is a viral disease that primarily affects the reproductive and respiratory systems of pigs.
- It can result in reproductive failure, respiratory distress, and increased susceptibility to secondary infections.
- Vaccination and strict biosecurity practices are common methods of prevention.

Swine Influenza (Flu):

- Swine flu is caused by various influenza A viruses that affect pigs.
- It can lead to respiratory symptoms, reduced growth rates, and increased mortality, especially in young pigs.
- Vaccination may be used to reduce the impact of swine influenza.

Porcine Epidemic Diarrhea (PED):

- PED is a viral disease that causes severe diarrhea and dehydration in pigs, particularly in piglets.
- It can result in high mortality rates among newborn piglets.
- Strict hygiene and biosecurity measures are essential for prevention.

Classical Swine Fever (CSF):

- CSF, also known as hog cholera, is a viral disease that affects pigs and can lead to severe clinical signs, including high fever, loss of appetite, and hemorrhages.
- Vaccination is available in some regions, but control measures also involve quarantine and culling of affected animals.

Transmissible Gastroenteritis (TGE):

- TGE is a highly contagious viral disease that affects the gastrointestinal tract of pigs.
- It causes severe diarrhea and can lead to dehydration, especially in piglets.
- Biosecurity measures and hygiene practices are key for prevention.

Porcine Circovirus (PCV2):

- PCV2 is associated with various clinical syndromes collectively known as porcine circovirus-associated diseases (PCVAD).
- Clinical signs include wasting, respiratory distress, and diarrhea.
- Vaccination is commonly used for PCV2 control.

Actinobacillus Pleuropneumonia (APP):

- APP is a bacterial infection that causes severe pleuropneumonia in pigs.
- Infected pigs may exhibit respiratory distress, fever, and coughing.
- Control measures include vaccination and management practices.

Salmonellosis:

- Various Salmonella strains can affect pigs, leading to symptoms such as diarrhea, fever, and abortion in sows.
- Prevention involves good hygiene practices and proper sanitation.

It's essential for pig farmers to work closely with veterinarians and implement strict biosecurity measures to prevent the introduction and spread of these diseases on their farms. Vaccination, quarantine, and isolation protocols are also essential components of disease prevention and control in pig farming.

PREVENTING PIG DISEASES

Preventing pig diseases is a critical aspect of successful pig farming. Disease outbreaks can have devastating consequences, leading to economic losses, reduced pig health, and even the culling of infected animals. To maintain a healthy pig herd and minimize disease risks, here are key strategies for disease prevention:

Biosecurity Measures:

- **Restricted Access**: Limit access to your pig farm to authorized personnel only. Implement controlled entry and exit points to prevent unauthorized visitors and vehicles.

- **Quarantine**: Quarantine newly introduced pigs for a specific period (typically 30 days) in a separate isolation area. Monitor them for signs of illness before introducing them to the main herd.
- **Footbaths and Disinfection**: Provide footbaths with disinfectants at farm entrances to reduce the risk of introducing pathogens on footwear.
- **Protective Clothing**: Require all farm personnel and visitors to wear clean, farm-specific clothing and footwear, which should not be worn off the farm.
- **Equipment Sanitization**: Regularly clean and disinfect equipment, tools, and vehicles that come into contact with pigs.
- **Isolation Facilities**: Maintain isolation facilities for sick or potentially infected pigs to prevent the spread of diseases within the herd.

Health Monitoring:

- **Regular Health Checks**: Conduct regular health checks on all pigs in your herd. Look for signs of illness, lameness, or abnormal Behaviour.
- **Record Keeping**: Maintain detailed health records, including vaccination history, treatment protocols, and disease incidence. This information can help identify trends and respond to outbreaks effectively.
- **Veterinary Consultation**: Establish a relationship with a veterinarian who specializes in swine health. Regular consultations and advice from a professional are invaluable for disease prevention and management.
- **Vaccination Programs**: Ensure that all pigs receive the necessary vaccinations, boosters, and follow-up doses according to the recommended schedule.

Nutrition and Hygiene:

- Provide balanced nutrition to maintain the health and immunity of your pigs.
- Ensure that feed and water sources are clean and uncontaminated.
- Regularly clean and sanitize feeding equipment and waterers to prevent disease transmission through contaminated feed and water.

Environmental Management:

- Maintain clean and well-ventilated pig housing facilities.
- Properly dispose of pig waste to prevent contamination of the environment and water sources.
- Implement fly and pest control measures to reduce disease vectors.

Isolation and Treatment:

- Promptly isolate sick pigs to prevent the spread of disease within the herd.
- Seek veterinary assistance for accurate diagnosis and treatment of diseases.

Education and Training:

- Continuously educate yourself and your farm staff about pig health, disease prevention, and biosecurity measures.
- Stay informed about the latest developments in swine health and disease control.

Transportation Protocols:

- Ensure that vehicles used for transporting pigs are clean and disinfected before and after use.
- Follow strict loading and unloading protocols to minimize stress and disease transmission during transportation.
- Participate in disease surveillance programs and reporting systems established by local veterinary authorities.
- Be vigilant for signs of notifiable or reportable diseases and report them promptly to relevant authorities.

Preventing pig diseases requires a proactive and systematic approach, with an emphasis on biosecurity, monitoring, and veterinary care. By implementing these strategies, pig farmers can reduce the risk of disease outbreaks and maintain a healthy and productive pig herd.

CHAPTER 10
ADDRESSING COMMON NUTRITIONAL ISSUES IN PIG FARMING

PROPER NUTRITION IS a cornerstone of successful pig farming. Meeting the nutritional needs of your pigs is essential for growth, reproduction, and overall health. In this chapter, we will explore common nutritional issues in pig farming and strategies to address them effectively.

Balancing Nutrient Requirements

Protein and Amino Acids

- **Issue**: Inadequate or imbalanced protein in pig diets can lead to poor growth, reduced feed efficiency, and reproductive problems.
- **Solution**: Formulate diets to meet specific protein and amino acid requirements based on the pig's age, weight, and production stage. Utilize quality protein sources like soybean meal and fishmeal.

Energy

- **Issue**: Insufficient energy intake can hinder growth and reduce reproductive performance.
- **Solution**: Ensure diets provide the right level of energy through appropriate carbohydrate sources like cassava, corn, wheat, and barley. Adjust energy levels based on the pig's life stage and production goals.

Vitamins and Minerals

- **Issue**: Vitamin and mineral deficiencies can result in various health issues and reduced productivity.
- **Solution**: Formulate diets to include essential vitamins and minerals, either through natural feed ingredients or supplements. Regularly test feed and forages for nutrient content to make informed adjustments.

Feed Quality and Safety

Feed Contamination

- **Issue**: Contaminated feed can introduce toxins or pathogens, leading to health problems in pigs.
- **Solution**: Source feed from reputable suppliers, and implement strict quality control measures. Regularly test feed samples for contaminants and mycotoxins.

Feed Storage

- **Issue**: Improper feed storage can lead to spoilage, nutrient degradation, and the growth of harmful microorganisms.
- **Solution**: Store feed in clean, dry, and rodent-proof containers or silos. Use a first-in, first-out (FIFO) system to ensure freshness.

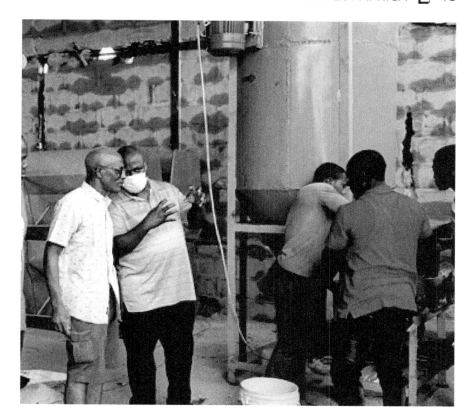

Water Quality

Poor Water Quality

- **Issue**: Contaminated or insufficient water can result in dehydration, reduced feed intake, and poor pig health.
- **Solution**: Always provide clean and uncontaminated water. Regularly clean waterers and pipes to maintain water quality.

Overfeeding or Underfeeding

- **Issue**: Incorrect feeding amounts can lead to wastage or inadequate nutrition.
- **Solution**: Follow feeding guidelines and adjust rations based on pig weight, age, and production stage. Monitor pig body condition regularly.

Feeder Design

- **Issue**: Poor feeder design can lead to feed wastage and inefficient feed conversion.
- **Solution**: Invest in well-designed feeders that minimize wastage and provide easy access to pigs.

Seasonal Feed Changes

- **Issue**: Seasonal variations in feed quality and availability can impact pig nutrition.
- **Solution**: Adjust diet formulations to account for seasonal changes in feed ingredients and quality.

Lack of Nutritional Knowledge

- **Issue**: Inadequate understanding of pig nutrition can lead to suboptimal diets.
- **Solution**: Continuously educate yourself and farm staff about pig nutrition through training programs and consultations with nutritionists.

Addressing common nutritional issues in pig farming requires a combination of sound nutrition knowledge, careful feed management, and quality control measures. By paying close attention to the nutritional needs of your pigs and implementing appropriate solutions, you can optimize growth, reproduction, and overall health in your pig herd. In the following chapters, we will delve deeper into pig health management, housing, and marketing strategies to further enhance your pig farming expertise.

TYPICAL FEED COMPOSITION

Pigs' dietary preferences have evolved, enabling them to adapt to various food sources, a key factor for their survival and evolutionary success. Early land-based animals, initially large amphibians, transitioned from consuming sea vertebrates to land vertebrates, becoming carnivorous. Some also started incorporating plant-based foods into their diets, turning herbivorous. Eventually, animals like pigs developed the capacity to consume plant and animal matter, classifying them as omnivores.

Unlike ruminants such as cattle and sheep, Pigs possess a simpler digestive system. Food enters the stomach through the oesophagus and subsequently moves into the small intestine for processing. While they cannot subsist solely on pasture like cattle or sheep, pigs can graze to some extent, provided they can access suitable plant species. Their ability to efficiently utilize cellulose and lignin sets pig digestion apart from humans. This is facilitated by their caecum, an organ attached to the large intestine, allowing for extended digestion of plant cell wall cellulose before it exits the pig's system. Although this organ is vital for herbivores, pigs, as omnivores, also benefit from its presence.

Pig feed resembles human food, consisting mainly of protein, carbohydrates, lipids (fats), minerals, vitamins, and water. The various local feed ingredients available for pig nutrition, such as Palm Kernel Cake, soy meal, Groundnut Cake, Maize, Fish Meal, Brewery waste, and Cassava, differ in nutrient composition. Some ingredients are richer in certain nutrients than others. For instance, legumes like soya and groundnut, as well as animal muscle tissues like fish and meat, contain higher protein levels but lower carbohydrate content compared to feed ingredients like sorghum, maize, wheat, cassava, yam, and potatoes, which are carbohydrate-rich and have lower protein content.

High-quality feed is essential for pig growth, body maintenance, and meat or milk production. Pigs exhibit rapid growth and reproductive rates compared to other domesticated livestock species, offering a higher meat yield per breeding female. As a pig farmer, your objective is to convert cost-effective feed ingredients into premium pork to produce high-quality, protein-rich food.

In the first four months of a pig's life, muscle tissue and skeletal bones develop faster than fat tissues. After this initial period, the trend reverses, with muscle development slowing down compared to fat. This explains why pigs can be fed ad libitum (as much as they can eat) up to a weight of 40 kg but require controlled rations in later production stages.

Feed consumed by pigs undergoes digestion within their bodies, with the absorbed nutrients contributing to their growth and maintenance. To optimize pig growth and production performance, feed should contain essential nutrients such as fibre, water, protein (including essential amino acids), carbohydrates, vitamins, minerals, salt, feed additives, and some essential fatty acids.

Cultivating Feed Crops for Swine Feeding

Pigs, being monogastric animals, can digest smaller quantities of green forages and leaves compared to cattle. Pig farmers can cultivate various food feed crops and forages (such as maize, sweet potatoes, cassava, and water spinach) near the pig pen at the homestead. Many of these crops can be grown as mixed crops in a small plot of land.

Cultivating feed crops has several advantages for pig farming:

- Cost-effectiveness
- Rich source of vitamins and minerals
- Significant protein contribution

- Reduced grain consumption
- Enhanced profit margins
- Improved pig health and productivity

In situations where concentrated feed is scarce or cash flow for feed is limited, crops like sweet potatoes, legume forages (e.g., watercress), mixed with broken rice (up to 20%), rice bran (15%), and a protein source (such as fish meal and oil cakes) can be combined to create a balanced pig feed. When using green leaves or vegetable forages, it's advisable to chop and boil them to enhance digestibility and reduce the risk of infectious diseases.

RECOMMENDED FOOD FEED CROPS FOR PIG FARMING

Here are some suggested food feed crops that pig farmers can cultivate for their swine. Many of these crops can be effectively grown as mixed crops in a small land plot.

Sweet Potatoes

- Suitable for various soil types, excluding clay, with sandy loam and deep loam being ideal, provided they have good drainage.
- Short vegetative cycle of 4-5 months, aligning well with cropping and pig production cycles.
- Yields more dry matter per hectare compared to cassava.
- Requires minimal cash input and limited horticultural practices.
- Exhibits good weed competitiveness among root and tuber crops.
- Cooking sweet potatoes enhances pig live-weight gain, with pigs grazing on sweet potatoes requiring a protein supplement of 500g concentrate per pig per day for optimal growth.

Cassava

- Grows on all soil types except saline, alkaline, and poorly drained soils.
- Thrives in hot and humid climates with well-distributed annual rainfall of 1,500 to 2,000mm.
- Can be profitably cultivated on hill slopes, waste land, and challenging cultivation areas.
- Ploughing or digging the land to a depth of 25 to 30cm is recommended.
- Irrigation is unnecessary with well-distributed rainfall.
- Cassava root can be used as dried cassava root (chips or pellets) for animal feed rations.
- Partial replacement of maize with cassava in young pig diets is cost-effective and sustainable, with up to 57% inclusion having no adverse effects on the pigs.
- Cassava leaves offer over 6 tonnes of crude protein per hectare per year, making them valuable for foliage harvesting.
- Cassava leaves are rich in crude protein, vitamins, and essential minerals.

Cocoyam

- Thrives in sandy loam soil and benefits from ploughing 2 to 3 times after applying organic manure and wood ash.
- "Earthen up" the soil around the plant when it reaches approximately 30cm in height.
- Cocoyam intended for pig feed must be cooked before drying and feeding to remove oxalic acid, a toxic substance present in corms, leaves, and petioles.
- Suitable for feeding sows in gestation and late lactation but not recommended for starter pigs or those in early growth stages.

Maize

- Requires well-drained soil selection and one ploughing followed by 2-3 harrowing sessions.
- Nitrogen application should be split into two doses, with the second dose applied 4 to 5 weeks after sowing.
- Irrigation helps maintain optimal soil moisture conditions, depending on rainfall intensity.
- One cutting in a year after 70 to 90 days of sowing yields optimal results.

Banana and Plantain

- These crops are staple foods in humid tropical regions, with bananas being the type commonly exported worldwide, while plantains are more locally utilized.
- Approximately 30–40% of total banana and plantain production can be directed towards livestock feeding due to rejection for export, accidental damage, domestic waste, etc.
- All parts of the banana and plantain plant can be used to feed pigs
- Fresh, green banana fruits with peels, either chopped or unchopped.
- Ripe, raw whole banana or plantain fruits.
- Dehydrated, sliced, milled, whole green bananas or plantains.
- Cooked, green, whole banana and plantain fruits.
- Dehydrated, milled, green and ripe plantain or banana peels.
- Chopped, fresh, green plantain and banana fruits ensiled with molasses, grass, legumes, rice bran, or other products to enhance their feeding value.

- Whole, fresh, green leaves, either fed directly to pigs or ensiled with easily fermentable carbohydrates like molasses.
- Banana and plantain stalks or pseudostems, chopped and fed raw or ensiled with easily fermentable carbohydrates like molasses.

For optimal digestibility and toxin breakdown, consider cooking various raw materials together, such as raw banana stem, maize, soya grains, beans, kitchen waste, and forage crops.

HYDROPONIC FODDER PRODUCTION ON A PIG FARM

Hydroponic Fodder Production is a sustainable and cost-effective method of growing feed for livestock, such as pigs, using a nutri-ent-rich water solution instead of soil.

This type of production offers many benefits, including reduced feed costs, higher feed quality and increased efficiency. In this method, seeds are sprouted in a controlled environment, producing a high-nutrient forage that is fed to pigs.

Hydroponic Fodder Production offers the ability to grow feed year-round, regardless of weather conditions and limited space and can be a sustainable option if you are looking to reduce your overall feed cost and your farm's environmental impact

Check our video to see our step-by-step process to achieve hydro-ponics on one of our farms in Imo state **Ezuhu Youth Pig Farm - commercial hydroponics - YouTube or enter on YouTube Papayemo1 hydroponics**

> **Step 1:** Choose the Right Space: Hydroponic systems require a lot of light, so choose a space that has ample natural light or can be supplemented with artificial light.

Make sure the space has enough room for the hydroponic setup.

Step 2: Prepare the Hydroponic System: Clean the hydroponic system thoroughly

Step 3: Choose the Right Plants : Select plants that are high in nutrients and are suitable for your pigs' dietary needs. Some popular choices for hydroponic systems include maize, millet, sorghum and soya bean

Step 4: Fill the Hydroponic System with Water: Fill the hydroponic system with water, making sure to use water that is free of chlorine and other chemicals.

Step 5: Start the Plants : Add seeds to the hydroponic system, and ensure that the plants receive proper lighting and nutrients. One kg of maize should give you 4 to 5 kg of hydroponic fodder.

Step 6: Introduce your Pigs : Once the plants have started to grow, introduce your pigs to the hydroponic system. Observe their behaviour and make any necessary adjustments to ensure they are comfortable and can access the plants easily.

Pristine Integrated Farm Resource Ltd has over 130 videos on different aspect of videos on pig production. We would recommend that you watch as many of possible especially this ones below as it would assist your farm productivity.

https://www.youtube.com/results?search_query=papayemo1+

- Pig Farm 14 - Feeding Your Pigs for Less Part 1 - YouTube

- Pig Farm 15 - Feeding Your Pigs for Less Part 2 - YouTube
- Ezuhu pig farm - Processing cassava for pig feed - YouTube
- Ezuhu Youth Pig Farm - commercial hydroponics – YouTube

CHAPTER 11
PIG FARM ROUTINE

QUOTE ON PIG FARMING PHILOSOPHY:

"The animals on the farm should be viewed as living factories, constantly converting their feed into products useful to humans. A fact of great economic importance is that a large part of the food they consume is of such a nature that humans cannot directly utilize it themselves."

HENRY AND MORISON IN FEED AND
FEEDING.

Pig management transcends mere pig raising; it involves navigating variable seasonal factors, fluctuating markets, and declining trade terms. The most successful pig farmers profoundly understand market dynamics, aligning product quality accordingly.

Numerous factors dictate the productivity and profitability of a pig enterprise:

1. Feedstuffs Supply and Quality
2. Appropriate Genetics Utilization
3. High Health Standards Maintenance
4. Optimal Housing and Environmental Conditions
5. Meeting Quality Assurance Requirements
6. Comprehensive Market Knowledge

The emergence of middle-class pig farmers underscores the need for commercial pig farming to adopt a business-oriented approach. Progress should be measured by profitability, not just physical performance. Successful commercial farmers must refine their management skills for better decision-making and resource allocation.

Pig management entails "making decisions to increase profits," efficiently employing available resources, and judiciously allocating them. These decisions hinge on the proprietor's goals, resource availability (e.g., land, labour, capital), and the diversity of potential resource applications.

A commercial pig farmer, therefore, wears dual hats—nurturing pigs and acting as a business manager. They make daily decisions, such as breed selection, resource utilization, production methods (e.g., intensive or free-range), and sales strategies.

However, pig farmers should recognize that, like all businesses, they operate within a dynamic and evolving environment:

- **Changing Prices**: Input and output prices fluctuate based on supply, demand, and market forces, impacting farm profitability.

- **Shifting Resource Availability**: The quantity and availability of inputs, such as grains, influence farm economics.
- **Evolving Technical Relationships**: Advances in technology alter the input-output dynamics, affecting profitability decisions.
- **Altering Institutional/Social Relations**: Government policies and banking support may influence expansion decisions and target markets.

TYPICAL PITFALLS FOR NEW PIG FARMERS:

New pig farmers are often dedicated and hardworking but can fall into common pitfalls:

- Inadequate understanding of pig production fundamentals.
- Poor record-keeping and measurement.
- Overconfidence due to experience.
- Underestimating the complexity of pig production.
- Lack of observation and adaptability.
- Overwhelming workload with limited strategic thinking.
- Reliance on unverified individuals.
- Overstocking and inadequate growth monitoring.
- Overinvestment in fixed assets.
- Inefficient resource use.
- Inadequate labour recruitment and training.
- Hasty breeding decisions.
- Underutilizing veterinary services.
- Resistance to partnerships and collaboration.
- Neglecting biosecurity.
- Insufficient business perspective.
- Ignoring the impact of mycotoxins.
- Poor prioritization of investments.
- Delaying necessary expenditures.

FARM MANAGER'S TIME ALLOCATION:

A farm manager's time should be distributed as follows:

1. Inspect every pig pen daily.
2. Update farm records daily.
3. Review farm finances weekly.
4. Identify cost-saving opportunities.
5. Monitor pig growth.
6. Conduct daily staff briefings.
7. Plan and explore marketing strategies.
8. Investigate new feed sources.
9. Supervise weekly pig feed composition.

PRIORITY OF A PIG FARM MANAGER:

The primary focus of a farm manager includes:

- Effective pig sales: Facilitating easy access for consumers, middlemen, processors, or retail outlets to purchase pigs of the required quality, timely and at minimal cost.
- Cost control: Managing productivity to maximize profits by redirecting resources effectively.
- Capital investment: Prioritizing investments in precision feeding, disease control, and environmental management, ensuring substantial returns.
- Delegating farm chores: Avoiding excessive manual labor to maintain focus on crucial management areas.
- Profit orientation: Shifting from output-centric thinking to profit-maximizing strategies.
- Recruitment and training: Employing an adequate workforce and providing professional training to optimize farm operations.

Managing a pig farm involves a daily and weekly routine to ensure the health, well-being, and productivity of the pigs. Here is a typical daily and weekly schedule for activities on a pig farm:

Daily Routine:

1. **Feeding**: Pigs typically require two meals a day. Feed them a balanced diet to meet their nutritional needs. Adjust feed quantities based on their age, weight, and production stage.
2. **Watering**: Ensure that pigs have access to clean, fresh water at all times. Check waterers for cleanliness and functionality.
3. **Health Monitoring**: Observe pigs for any signs of illness or distress. Check for lameness, abnormal behaviours, or injuries. Isolate and treat sick pigs promptly.
4. **Housing Inspection**: Inspect pig housing for cleanliness, ventilation, and temperature control. Ensure that bedding is clean and dry.
5. **Cleaning**: Remove manure and soiled bedding from pens and housing areas. Proper waste management is essential for disease prevention.
6. **Exercise and Enrichment**: Allow pigs time for exercise and exploration. Provide environmental enrichment, such as toys or rooting materials, to prevent boredom.
7. **Record-Keeping**: Maintain accurate records of feed consumption, pig health, and any notable observations. Good record-keeping is essential for farm management.
8. **Breeding and Reproduction**: If you have breeding sows, monitor their oestrus cycle and breeding activities. Keep detailed records of breeding dates.
9. **Weaning**: If piglets are ready for weaning, follow a weaning schedule based on their age and weight. Transition them to a post-weaning diet.

10. **Biosecurity Measures**: Follow biosecurity protocols to prevent the introduction and spread of diseases. Implement measures like footbaths and controlled access to the farm.

Weekly Routine:

1. **Vaccinations and Medications**: Administer vaccinations and medications as required. Follow a vaccination schedule recommended by a veterinarian.
2. **Housing Maintenance**: Conduct weekly checks of housing structures for wear and tear. Repair any damaged components promptly.
3. **Weighing**: Weigh pigs weekly to monitor growth rates and adjust feed rations accordingly. Record weights for each pig.
4. **Feed Inventory**: Keep track of feed inventory to ensure you have enough feed on hand. Order additional feed as needed to avoid shortages.
5. **Market Preparation**: If you are selling pigs for market, plan for their transportation and processing. Ensure they meet the desired market weight and quality standards.
6. **Farrowing Management**: If you have farrowing sows, inspect farrowing crates and ensure proper care for newborn piglets. Record the number of piglets born and monitor their health.
7. **Cleaning and Sanitization**: Conduct a thorough cleaning of housing facilities, equipment, and feeding troughs to maintain a hygienic environment.
8. **Record Review**: Review weekly records to identify trends or issues that may require attention. Use the data to make informed management decisions.
9. **Staff Training**: Provide ongoing training to farm staff on pig care, handling, and biosecurity practices.

10. **Farm Planning**: Evaluate farm performance and make adjustments to production goals, breeding plans, and marketing strategies based on your observations and market conditions.

It's important to note that the specific activities and their timing may vary depending on the scale and type of pig farming operation, as well as regional climate and disease considerations. Regular communication with a veterinarian or agricultural extension officer can provide valuable guidance in developing and maintaining a successful routine on a pig farm.

Farm Inspection

Housing inspection is a critical aspect of pig farming that ensures the well-being and productivity of your pigs. Regular inspections help identify and address issues related to cleanliness, ventilation, temperature control, and overall housing conditions. Here's a guideline for conducting housing inspections on a pig farm:

Frequency: Housing inspections should be conducted daily, ideally in the morning and evening, and more comprehensive weekly inspections can be carried out.

Tools Needed:

- Clean and appropriate work attire, including boots and coveralls.
- A notepad or digital device for recording observations.
- Adequate lighting, especially if inspecting during dark hours.

Areas to Inspect:

- **Overall Cleanliness:** Check for accumulated manure and soiled bedding in pens or housing areas. Remove any waste to maintain a clean and hygienic environment.

- **Ventilation:** Verify that air circulation is sufficient to prevent the buildup of moisture and harmful gases like ammonia.
- **Temperature Control:** Monitor the temperature inside housing facilities.
- **Bedding:** Inspect bedding materials for cleanliness and dryness. Replace bedding if it is soiled or damp to prevent discomfort and health issues.
- **Water Supply:** Check waterers to ensure they are clean and functioning properly. Verify that pigs have continuous access to clean, fresh water.
- **Lighting:** Ensure that lighting levels are appropriate for pig behaviour, growth, and reproductive performance.
- **Feeders:** Inspect feeders for cleanliness and functionality. Ensure that feed is available to pigs as scheduled.
- **Structural Integrity:** Examine the structural integrity of housing facilities, including walls, roofs, and flooring. Repair any damage or wear and tear promptly to prevent safety hazards.
- **Security:** Verify that housing areas are secure and free from potential hazards or points of escape. Check gates and fencing for integrity.
- **Enrichment and Comfort:** Ensure that environmental enrichment materials (e.g., toys or rooting materials) are accessible to pigs. Verify that pigs have enough space to move, rest, and perform natural behaviours.
- **Health and Behaviour:** Observe pigs for any signs of illness or abnormal behaviour during the inspection. Take note of any pigs that may require isolation or medical attention.
- **Record-Keeping:** Record any observations, maintenance tasks, or issues identified during the inspection. Maintain a log of housing conditions to track trends and improvements over time.

- **Immediate Action:** If you discover any urgent issues during the inspection, such as sick or injured pigs or structural damage, take immediate action to address them. This may involve isolating sick pigs, repairing facilities, or notifying a veterinarian for assistance.

Regular housing inspections are crucial for maintaining a healthy and productive pig herd. They help prevent disease outbreaks, ensure pig comfort, and contribute to the overall success of your pig farming operation.

CASTRATION OF PIGS

Castration, the surgical removal of a pig's testicles, is a common practice in the swine industry for various reasons. This procedure is often performed on male piglets at a young age, typically between 1 and 7 days old. While castration remains a practical necessity for many pig farmers, it has become a subject of controversy and debate due to ethical concerns. In this section, we will explore the reasons for pig castration, the methods employed, and the ethical considerations surrounding this practice.

Reasons for Pig Castration:

1. **Reducing Aggression and Boar Taint:** Uncastrated male pigs, known as boars, are prone to aggressive behaviour, including fighting and mounting other pigs. They may also develop a condition called "boar taint," which results in an unpleasant odor and taste in the pork meat. Castrating boars helps mitigate these issues, making it easier to manage pigs in group housing and improving meat quality.
2. **Improved Meat Quality:** Castrated male pigs, known as barrows, produce pork with consistent and desirable flavor characteristics. This leads to higher consumer

acceptance and fewer instances of pork being rejected due to boar taint.

3. **Animal Welfare and Handling:** Aggressive boars can pose a risk to farm workers and other pigs. Castrating male piglets reduces aggressive Behaviours, making it safer for both humans and animals during handling and transportation.

Methods of Pig Castration:

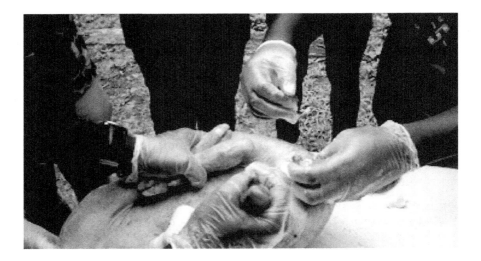

There are several methods of pig castration, including:

Surgical Castration: This method involves making small incisions in the scrotum, removing the testicles, and closing the incisions with sutures or clips. Surgical castration is typically performed by a trained farm personnel using sterile equipment.

Ethical Considerations:

Pig castration has sparked ethical concerns, primarily related to animal welfare. Critics argue that castration causes pain and distress to piglets, and there is a growing call for alternative practices that minimize these negative impacts. Some of the ethical considerations include:

1. **Pain and Stress:** Surgical castration, in particular, can cause pain and stress to piglets, even when performed with anaesthesia and analgesia. Critics argue that more effective pain management techniques should be employed.
2. **Age and Timing:** Performing castration at a young age may be less traumatic than doing it when pigs are older. Early castration can minimize stress and discomfort for piglets.

Step-by-Step Process of Pig Castration

1. **Preparation:** Before beginning the castration process, it's crucial to ensure a clean and sanitary environment. Sterilize all equipment, including surgical instruments, to minimize the risk of infection. Gather necessary supplies, such as gloves, antiseptic solution, scissors or scalpel, and sutures or clips (if performing surgical castration).
2. **Selection of Piglets:** Identify the piglets that are suitable for castration. This is typically done within the first week of life when piglets are still young and small. Choose piglets that are healthy and free from signs of illness.
3. **Restraint:** Piglets should be properly restrained to ensure safety during the procedure. Hold the piglet securely but gently to prevent excessive movement.

Surgical Castration:

a. **Incision:** If performing surgical castration, make small incisions on each side of the scrotum using scissors or a scalpel. The incisions should be large enough to allow access to the testicles but not too extensive to minimize bleeding.

b. **Testicle Removal:** Gently manipulate each testicle to expose the spermatic cord. Sever the spermatic cord using scissors or a scalpel, ensuring minimal bleeding. Remove the testicle and repeat the process on the other side.

c. **Closure:** Close the incisions with sutures or clips to prevent infection. Ensure that the sutures or clips are secure but not too tight to avoid constriction.

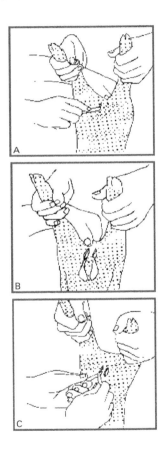

Post-Castration Care:

a. **Pain Management:** Continue to provide pain relief to piglets as needed post-castration, as they may experience discomfort for a period after the procedure.

b. **Observation:** Observe the castrated piglets for signs of infection, excessive bleeding, or other complications. Any issues should be addressed promptly.

1. **Record Keeping:** Maintain records of castrated piglets, including their identification, date of castration, and any complications or treatments administered. Good record-keeping helps with farm management and traceability.
2. **Weaning and Growing:** After castration, piglets should be allowed to recover and grow in a suitable environment with proper nutrition and care.
3. **Continued Monitoring:** Keep a watchful eye on castrated piglets as they grow to ensure their health and well-being.

It's essential to emphasize the importance of responsible and humane castration practices in pig farming. Proper pain management, early castration, and adherence to best practices contribute to minimizing the potential discomfort and stress experienced by piglets during and after the procedure. Moreover, continuous research and development in this field aim to find more humane alternatives to traditional physical castration methods.

ADMINISTERING INTRAMUSCULAR INJECTIONS IN PIGS

Administering intramuscular (IM) injections to pigs is a common veterinary procedure in swine farming. Whether it's for vaccination, medication, or other therapeutic purposes, proper injection technique is vital to ensure the well-being and health of the animals. This section explores the process of administering intramuscular injections in pigs, highlighting best practices, safety measures, and the importance of precise execution.

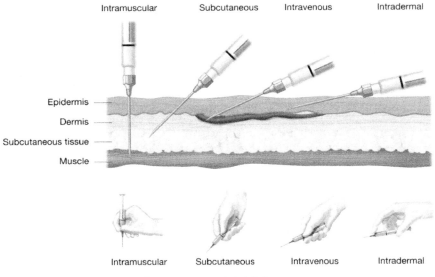

Source: www.minipiginfo.com

Why Intramuscular Injections in Pigs?

Intramuscular injections are chosen for specific medications or vaccines that need to be absorbed quickly and efficiently into the bloodstream. Pigs, like many animals, have well-developed muscles that provide an ideal site for IM injections. Administering medication through this route ensures accurate dosing and facilitates rapid absorption.

Best Practices for Administering IM Injections in Pigs:

1. **Equipment and Preparation:** Before starting the procedure, gather the necessary equipment, including syringes, needles, medication, alcohol swabs, and appropriate safety gear. Ensure that the equipment is clean and sterile.

2. **Proper Restraint:** Pigs can be strong and potentially unpredictable. Secure the pig in a safe and comfortable position to minimize stress and the risk of injury to both

the animal and the operator. Gentle restraint techniques are preferred.

3. **Site Selection:** Choose the injection site carefully. Common IM injection sites in pigs include the neck, the muscles behind the ear, or the hamstrings. The chosen area should be free from any visible signs of infection or injury.

4. **Needle Size and Length:** Select an appropriate needle size and length based on the pig's age, size, and the type of medication. The needle should be long enough to reach the muscle but not so long that it penetrates through the muscle.

5. **Cleanliness:** Clean the injection site with an alcohol swab to reduce the risk of infection. Allow the site to dry before administering the injection.

6. **Technique:** Hold the syringe and needle at a 90-degree angle to the skin. Steadily insert the needle into the selected muscle. Avoid sudden movements that may cause the pig discomfort or injury.

7. **Aspiration:** Before injecting the medication, aspirate (pull back on the plunger) to check for blood in the syringe. If blood is present, it may indicate that the needle is in a blood vessel, and you should reposition it.

8. **Slow and Steady Injection:** Administer the medication slowly and steadily to ensure accurate dosing. Avoid injecting too quickly, as it may cause discomfort or tissue damage.

9. **Withdraw Needle:** After injecting the medication, withdraw the needle gently and quickly to minimize discomfort to the pig. Apply light pressure to the injection site with a sterile cotton ball or gauze pad to prevent leakage.

10. **Dispose of Sharps Safely:** Properly dispose of used needles and syringes in designated sharps containers to prevent injury and contamination.

Post-Injection Care:

After administering the IM injection, observe the pig for any adverse reactions or complications. Ensure that the pig remains in a clean and comfortable environment to facilitate recovery.

Administering intramuscular injections in pigs is a routine but essential aspect of swine management. Proper technique, equipment, and hygiene are crucial to ensure the health and well-being of the animals. When performed correctly, IM injections are an effective means of delivering medications and vaccines, contributing to the overall health and productivity of pig farming operations. It is essential for pig farmers and farm personnel to receive training and guidance from veterinarians or experienced professionals to master the art of administering IM injections in pigs safely and efficiently.

ADMINISTERING SUBCUTANEOUS INJECTIONS

Subcutaneous (SC) injections are commonly used in veterinary medicine to administer medications, vaccines, or therapeutic substances to animals, including pigs. This non-intrusive route of administration allows for the gradual absorption of the substance and is suitable for various treatments. In this section, we will outline the step-by-step process of administering subcutaneous injections in pigs, emphasizing best practices and safety measures.

Why Subcutaneous Injections in Pigs?

Subcutaneous injections are chosen for certain medications or vaccines that require a slower release into the bloodstream. The subcutaneous tissue, located just beneath the skin, allows for the gradual absorption of the substance while avoiding the need to penetrate muscles, making it a less painful and more convenient option for both the pig and the operator.

Step-by-Step Process of Administering Subcutaneous Injections in Pigs:

1. **Gather Supplies:** Before starting the procedure, gather all the necessary supplies, including a syringe, an appropriate needle, the medication or vaccine, alcohol swabs, and safety gear such as gloves.
2. **Restrain the Pig:** Secure the pig in a safe and comfortable position to minimize stress and ensure safety for both the animal and the operator. Gentle restraint techniques are preferable to avoid undue stress.
3. **Select the Injection Site:** Choose an appropriate injection site for subcutaneous administration. Common sites in pigs include the loose skin on the neck, behind the ear, or in the flank area. Ensure that the chosen area is free from signs of infection or injury.
4. **Needle Size and Length:** Select the appropriate needle size and length based on the pig's age, size, and the type of medication. A 20- to 22-gauge needle, approximately 3/4 to 1.5 inches long, is typically suitable for subcutaneous injections in pigs.
5. **Cleanliness:** Clean the injection site using an alcohol swab. Allow the site to dry before administering the injection to prevent contamination.
6. **Technique:** Hold the syringe and needle at a 45-degree angle to the skin. Gently pinch a small fold of skin between your thumb and forefinger to create a tent-like area.
7. **Insert the Needle:** Insert the needle into the subcutaneous tissue within the fold of skin. Ensure that you maintain the proper angle and depth, so the needle is fully inserted into the subcutaneous space.
8. **Aspiration:** Before injecting the medication or vaccine, aspirate (pull back on the plunger) to check for blood in

the syringe. If blood is present, it may indicate that the needle is in a blood vessel, and you should reposition it.

9. **Slow and Steady Injection:** Administer the medication or vaccine slowly and steadily to ensure accurate dosing. Avoid injecting too quickly, as this may cause discomfort or tissue damage.

10. **Withdraw Needle:** After administering the substance, withdraw the needle gently and quickly to minimize discomfort to the pig. Apply light pressure to the injection site with a sterile cotton ball or gauze pad to prevent leakage.

11. **Dispose of Sharps Safely:** Properly dispose of used needles and syringes in designated sharps containers to prevent injury and contamination.

Post-Injection Care:

After administering the subcutaneous injection, observe the pig for any adverse reactions or complications. Ensure that the pig remains in a clean and comfortable environment to facilitate recovery.

TAKING THE TEMPERATURE OF PIGS

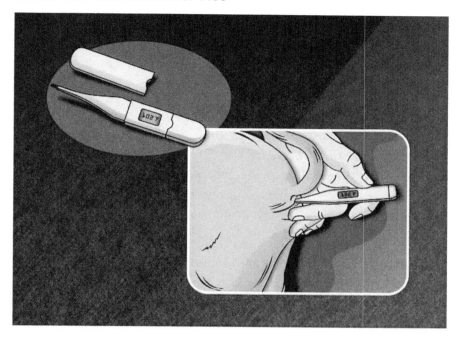

Taking the temperature of pigs is a crucial aspect of pig farming and animal health management. Monitoring their body temperature provides valuable insights into their health and can help identify potential issues or illnesses early on. Here are some important points to consider when taking the temperature of pigs:

Tools for Temperature Measurement: The most common method for taking a pig's temperature is to use a rectal thermometer designed for veterinary use. Digital thermometers are recommended for their accuracy and ease of use.

Prepare the Environment: Ensure that the pig is in a calm and secure environment to minimize stress during the process. Wear appropriate personal protective equipment (PPE) such as gloves to prevent the spread of diseases and to ensure safety for both the pig and the person taking the temperature.

Technique: Lubricate the thermometer with a water-soluble lubricant to facilitate easy insertion. Gently lift the pig's tail and insert the thermometer into the rectum, being cautious not to force it. Insert it about 1.5 to 2 inches (3.8 to 5 cm) deep. Hold the thermometer in place for at least one minute to get an accurate reading.

Normal Temperature Range: The normal body temperature for pigs can vary slightly based on their age and size but generally falls within the range of 101.5°F to 103.5°F (38.6°C to 39.7°C).. If a pig's temperature falls outside the normal range or if there are other signs of illness such as lethargy, loss of appetite, or abnormal behaviour, consult a veterinarian for a proper diagnosis and treatment.

In conclusion, taking a pig's temperature is a routine but essential practice in pig farming. Regular temperature monitoring can aid in the early detection of health issues, allowing for timely intervention and improved overall herd health. It's essential to conduct this procedure with care, using proper equipment and hygiene practices to ensure the well-being of the animals and farm personnel.

CHAPTER 12
SELECTING GILTS FOR YOUR FARM

THE SELECTION of gilts is a crucial process in swine farming that forms the foundation of a productive and healthy herd. Gilts, young female pigs that have not yet given birth, are the future breeding stock of a pig farm. The decision to choose the right gilts directly impacts the genetic potential, health, and overall success of a swine operation. In this section, we will delve into the significance of selecting gilts, the criteria for their evaluation, and the steps involved in this critical process.

The Importance of Selecting Gilts:

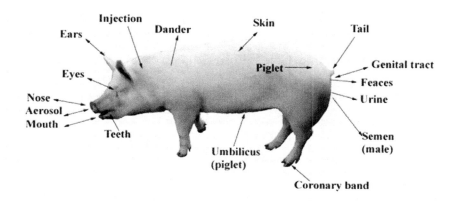

Genetic Improvement: Selecting the right gilts allows pig farmers to improve the genetic characteristics of their herd. Careful selection can enhance traits such as growth rate, meat quality, disease resistance, and reproductive efficiency, leading to higher productivity and profitability. Disease-free gilts contribute to a healthier overall herd, reducing the need for medication and veterinary interventions.

Long-Term Productivity: Gilts are expected to serve as breeding sows for several years. Proper selection ensures the long-term productivity and sustainability of the breeding herd, which is essential for consistent pork production.

Criteria for Evaluating Gilts:

When selecting gilts for your farm, consider the following criteria:

1. **Conformation and Structure:** Examine the gilts' overall conformation and body structure. They should have a balanced body shape, good muscling, and well-defined reproductive organs.
2. **Health and Vitality:** Ensure that gilts are healthy, free from diseases, and have a strong immune system. Look for signs of illness, lameness, or respiratory issues.
3. **Reproductive History:** If available, review the reproductive history of the gilt's parents and lineage. Select gilts from sows and boars with a history of high fertility and successful litters.
4. **Weight and Size:** Consider the gilt's weight and size. They should be in good body condition but not overly fat or underweight. A body condition score of 3 or 4 is ideal.
5. **Age:** Select gilts that are at the appropriate age for breeding. They should be around 6 to 8 months old and have reached sexual maturity.
6. **Temperament:** Observe the temperament of the gilts. Docile and easy-to-handle gilts are preferable, as they are

less likely to exhibit aggressive behaviour or stress-related issues.

Steps in Selecting Gilts:

1. **Identify Your Breeding Goals:** Determine the specific breeding goals for your farm, such as improving growth rates, meat quality, or disease resistance. These goals will guide your selection process.
2. **Source Gilts from Reputable Suppliers:** Acquire gilts from reputable breeders or suppliers known for high-quality breeding stock. Conduct thorough background checks and request health certificates.
3. **Conduct Physical Examinations:** Physically examine each gilt to assess their overall health, body condition, and conformation. Look for any signs of lameness, injuries, or abnormalities.
4. **Review Lineage and Records:** If available, review the lineage and performance records of the gilts' parents and ancestors. This information can provide insights into their genetic potential.
5. **Quarantine and Health Testing:** Quarantine new gilts upon arrival to the farm and conduct health testing to ensure they are free from diseases. Isolate them from the existing herd during this period.
6. **Observe Behavioural Traits:** Pay attention to the behaviour and temperament of the gilts. Select gilts that are calm, easy to handle, and show good adaptability to the farm environment.
7. **Maintain Records:** Keep detailed records of each selected gilt, including their source, age, weight, health status, and any other relevant information.

The selection of gilts is a critical process that significantly influences the future success of a swine farm. Careful evaluation based on criteria such as conformation, health, reproductive history, and temperament ensures that the chosen gilts will contribute to a genetically superior, healthy, and productive breeding herd. By setting clear breeding goals and following best practices in the selection process, pig farmers can establish a strong foundation for swine production and achieve long-term success in their operations.

MANAGING GILTS ON YOUR FARM

The management of gilts on a swine farm is a crucial aspect of successful swine production. Gilts, young female pigs that have not yet given birth, represent the future breeding stock of the herd. Proper management from selection through to breeding and farrowing ensures the health, productivity, and genetic advancement of the herd. In this section, we will explore the importance of managing gilts, key aspects of gilt management, and best practices for nurturing them on your farm.

The Significance of Managing Gilts:

1. **Genetic Improvement:** Gilts are the conduit for genetic progress within a swine herd. Careful management allows pig farmers to select and develop breeding stock that exhibits desired traits such as growth rate, meat quality, disease resistance, and reproductive efficiency.
2. **Reproductive Efficiency:** Efficient gilt management ensures that gilts are bred at the right time, in optimal condition, and with a high likelihood of successful farrowing. This enhances the breeding herd's productivity.
3. **Disease Prevention:** Proactive management practices help prevent the introduction of diseases or pathogens to the gilt population, which can have a detrimental impact on the entire herd.

Key Aspects of Gilt Management:

1. **Nutrition:** Provide gilts with a balanced and nutritionally appropriate diet to support growth and reproduction. Nutrition is crucial to achieving the right body condition for breeding.
2. **Health Care:** Implement a comprehensive health care program for gilts, including vaccinations, deworming, and regular health checks. Keep detailed health records to monitor their well-being.
3. **Housing:** Ensure that gilts have suitable housing that allows for comfort, ventilation, and protection from extreme weather conditions. Proper housing contributes to their overall health and reproductive success.
4. **Breeding Management:** Time breeding carefully to ensure that gilts are at the right age, weight, and condition. Monitor oestrus signs and manage breeding based on a gilt's reproductive readiness.

5. **Behavioural Management:** Monitor and manage the Behaviour of gilts within group housing to prevent aggression, stress, and injuries. Proper socialization is important.
6. **Reproductive Records:** Keep detailed records of each gilt's reproductive history, including breeding dates, pregnancy status, and farrowing outcomes. This information guides future breeding decisions.

Best Practices for Gilt Management:

1. **Nutrition Plan:** Develop a comprehensive nutrition plan tailored to the specific needs of gilts at different stages of development, including gestation and lactation.
2. **Socialization:** Manage group-housed gilts to ensure they adapt well to the social dynamics of the group. Minimize stressors and prevent aggression.
3. **Breeding Timing:** Use oestrus detection methods or consult with a veterinarian to ensure proper timing of breeding. Proper synchronization and management of breeding will enhance reproductive efficiency.
4. **Farrowing Preparedness:** Prepare gilts for farrowing by providing appropriate farrowing facilities, nesting materials, and veterinary support as needed.

Managing gilts on a swine farm is a multifaceted process that encompasses nutrition, health, housing, and reproductive management. The proper management of gilts is essential for the genetic progress, reproductive efficiency, and overall success of a swine production operation. By adhering to best practices and maintaining meticulous records, pig farmers can nurture a healthy and productive gilt population that serves as the cornerstone of their breeding herd, contributing to the long-term sustainability and profitability of the farm.

DETECTING SIGNS OF HEAT

Detecting signs of heat in a gilt, also known as oestrus, is essential for successful breeding. Gilt's display several behavioural and physical signs when they are in heat. Here are common signs to look for:

Behavioural Signs:

1. **Restlessness:** Gilt may appear restless, constantly moving around in the pen, and showing increased activity.
2. **Vocalization:** Gilt may become more vocal, often with a distinctive "calling" or "singing" sound to attract a boar's attention.
3. **Mounting Behaviour:** In some cases, gilts may mount other pigs, although this Behaviour is less common in gilts compared to sows.
4. **Immobilization Reflex:** When pressure is applied to the gilt's back, she may "freeze" or stand still. This is known as the immobilization reflex and is a sign that the gilt is receptive to mounting.

Physical Signs:

1. **Swollen Vulva:** The vulva becomes swollen and reddened during oestrus, making it more noticeable.
2. **Mucous Discharge:** Some gilts may have a clear or slightly cloudy mucous discharge from the vulva during oestrus.
3. **Increased Mounting:** While gilts are less likely to actively mount other pigs, they may stand still and allow other pigs, particularly boars, to mount them.
4. **Tail Flagging:** Some gilts may raise and twitch their tails when in the presence of a boar.
5. **Reddened Skin:** The skin around the vulva and udder may become redder and more vascularized.

6. **Sniffing and Flehmen Response:** Gilt may display interest in the scent of other pigs, especially boars, and exhibit the flehmen response, which involves curling the upper lip to detect pheromones in the air.

It's important to note that the intensity and duration of these signs can vary among individual gilts, and not all gilts will display all these signs. Monitoring gilt behaviour and physical changes is essential to determine the timing of oestrus accurately.

To maximize breeding success, it's crucial to identify these signs and plan mating during the gilt's oestrus period, typically lasting 2-3 days. Timing mating correctly is vital to ensure that the gilt is bred when she is most fertile, which is usually within 24 to 36 hours of the onset of oestrus. Proper record-keeping and observation are essential tools for managing gilt oestrus and successful breeding.

MATING A GILT

Mating a gilt, the process of introducing a young female pig to a boar for breeding, is a crucial step in swine production. The success of this process greatly influences the reproductive efficiency and genetic advancement of your swine herd. Here's a step-by-step guide on how to properly mate a gilt:

Preparation:

Age and Weight: Gilt should ideally be between 7 and 9 months old and weigh at least 180-220 pounds (80-100 kilograms). Provide a well-balanced and nutritionally adequate diet to ensure the gilt is in proper body condition for breeding. Gilt should have sufficient body fat to support reproduction.

Detection of Oestrus (Heat): Regularly observe the gilt for signs of oestrus, also known as "heat." Signs may include restlessness, swollen vulva, increased vocalization, and mounting other pigs.

Mating Process:

1. **Timing:** Timing is crucial. Gilt should be mated within 24 to 36 hours of the onset of oestrus, which is when she is most fertile. Oestrus typically lasts for 2-3 days.
2. **Supervision:** Supervise the mating process to ensure it occurs safely. Introduce the gilt to the boar in a controlled environment, such as a breeding pen.
3. **Boar Mating Behaviour:** Observe the boar's behaviour during mating. The boar will typically mount the gilt, display thrusting movements, and vocalize. These are signs of successful mating.
4. **Multiple Matings:** Allow for multiple mating sessions over a period of 2-3 days to increase the likelihood of conception.
5. **Record Keeping:** Keep detailed records of the mating process, including the dates and times of mating, the boar used, and any observations. This information is crucial for managing the gilt's pregnancy and farrowing.

Post-Mating Care:

1. **Separation:** After successful mating, remove the gilt from the presence of the boar to prevent over-mating, which can be physically stressful.
2. **Pregnancy Confirmation:** Monitor the gilt for signs of pregnancy, such as a lack of return to oestrus. Confirm pregnancy through ultrasound or a veterinarian's examination.
3. **Gestation Care:** If the gilt is confirmed pregnant, provide appropriate nutrition and care throughout the gestation period, which typically lasts around 114 days (3 months, 3 weeks, and 3 days).

4. **Farrowing Preparation:** As the gilt's due date approaches, prepare a clean and suitable farrowing area with nesting materials, water, and a heat source.

Mating a gilt is a crucial step in swine production that requires careful planning, timing, and monitoring. By following the proper steps and maintaining detailed records, pig farmers can increase the likelihood of successful breeding and the birth of healthy piglets. Effective gilt mating contributes to the genetic progress, reproductive efficiency, and overall success of a swine production operation.

CARE AND MANAGEMENT OF PREGNANT SOW

The care and management of pregnant sows are essential to ensure the well-being of the sow and the successful development of the piglets she is carrying. Proper management during pregnancy contributes to the overall health and productivity of the swine herd. Here's a comprehensive guide on how to care for and manage pregnant sows:

1. Nutrition:

- Provide a well-balanced diet formulated for pregnant sows. Adjust the feed to meet their nutritional requirements, which increase as pregnancy progresses.
- Ensure sows have access to clean, fresh water at all times.
- Monitor the body condition of pregnant sows to prevent excessive weight loss or obesity. Adjust their diet accordingly.

2. Housing:

- House pregnant sows in clean and comfortable pens or gestation stalls that allow them to stand, lie down, and turn around comfortably.

- Ensure proper ventilation to maintain good air quality and temperature control.
- Keep the housing area well-maintained, dry, and free from drafts.

3. Health Care:

- Develop a herd health program with a veterinarian to address vaccination, deworming, and disease prevention.
- Regularly monitor sows for signs of illness or discomfort, such as lameness, coughing, or abnormal Behaviours.
- Maintain a clean and hygienic environment to minimize the risk of disease transmission.

4. Monitoring:

- Monitor the pregnant sows' weight and body condition throughout pregnancy to ensure they are gaining weight appropriately.
- Record breeding dates and expected farrowing dates to facilitate management and care planning.

5. Gestation Length:

- The gestation period for sows is approximately 114 days (3 months, 3 weeks, and 3 days). Be prepared for farrowing around this time.

6. Farrowing Preparation:

- Prepare a clean and dry farrowing area equipped with appropriate nesting materials, such as straw or shavings.
- Ensure proper heating or heat lamps to maintain piglet comfort.

7. Farrowing Management:

- Monitor sows closely as they approach farrowing. Signs of impending farrowing include restlessness, nesting behaviour, and udder engorgement.
- Provide assistance during farrowing, if necessary, but allow the sow to assume most of the responsibilities.
- Record the number of piglets born and their health status.

8. Post-Farrowing Care:

- Ensure the sow and piglets are adequately bonded and that piglets are nursing.
- Administer any necessary vaccinations or treatments to the piglets, such as iron injections or ear notching for identification.
- Monitor the health of both the sow and piglets in the post-farrowing period.

9. Repeat Breeding:

- After weaning, ensure sows are on an appropriate diet to regain body condition.
- Implement a controlled breeding program to optimize the timing of the next pregnancy.

10. Record Keeping:

- Maintain detailed records of each sow's reproductive history, including breeding dates, farrowing dates, and health records.
- Use these records to make informed management decisions.

11. Proper Weaning:

- Wean piglets at around 3-4 weeks of age, depending on their weight and condition.
- Transition piglets to a starter diet and monitor their growth.

By following these guidelines and providing proper care and management for pregnant sows, you can optimize the health and productivity of your swine herd while ensuring the well-being of both the sows and their piglets. Consistent and attentive care throughout the gestation and farrowing process is essential for successful swine production.

UNDERSTANDING THE ROLE OF OXYTOCIN IN PIG FARMING

In the world of pig farming, the significance of oxytocin is well-known. But what exactly is oxytocin, and how does it influence the physiology of these animals during the crucial phases of farrowing and nursing? Let's delve into the role of oxytocin in pig farming and how to ensure the smooth operation of this intricate hormonal process.

To grasp this concept, we must first revisit the anatomy and physiology of pigs to comprehend the hormonal changes occurring within female pigs as farrowing approaches.

- **As farrowing approaches**, the brain initiates the production of a hormone called prostaglandin. Prostaglandin's primary role is to halt the production of progesterone, the hormone responsible for sustaining pregnancy.
- **Prostaglandin then triggers the release of oxytocin into the bloodstream**. Oxytocin is a hormone that serves two critical functions:

- It induces contractions in the smooth muscles of the milk glands, leading to milk letdown in female animals.
- It causes contractions in the uterus, facilitating the expulsion of piglets during farrowing.
- **Oxytocin production can also be stimulated** by actions such as your staff gently rubbing the sow's udder, mimicking the reflexes triggered by nursing piglets. This natural oxytocin release aids in the contractions necessary for pig delivery.
- **In some cases**, oxytocin injections may be employed to supplement the effects of naturally occurring oxytocin.

Guidelines to Avoid Improper Use of Oxytocin

Now, let's explore some essential guidelines to ensure the proper and safe use of oxytocin in pig farming:

1. **Timing is crucial**: Oxytocin injections should never be administered before the sow has delivered at least one piglet. Administering it prematurely can disrupt the normal farrowing process due to the stress it may induce.
2. **Use selectively**: Oxytocin should only be used in sows that appear to have ceased contractions before completing the delivery process.
3. **Avoid routine use**: Using oxytocin routinely can lead to increased stillbirths and other complications during farrowing.
4. **Thorough examination**: Always inspect the birth canal for any lodged piglets before administering oxytocin. Failure to clear obstructions can result in damage to the sow's uterus.
5. **Proper dosage**: If oxytocin is deemed necessary, administer one unit intramuscularly in the neck. Oxytocin acts swiftly, so excessive doses are not only wasteful but also potentially harmful to the sow.

6. **Monitor and repeat cautiously**: If required, repeat the oxytocin injection after 20 or 30 minutes. However, exercise caution to avoid overuse.

By following these guidelines, you can ensure the safe and effective use of oxytocin in pig farming, supporting healthy farrowing and nursing processes for your sows and piglets.

CARE OF THE NEW-BORN PIGLETS

The care of newborn piglets is critical to their survival and long-term health. Proper care during the first few weeks of life sets the foundation for their growth and development. Here are essential guidelines for caring for newborn piglets:

1. Warmth:

- Ensure that the farrowing area is warm and draft-free to prevent chilling of piglets. Use heat lamps or heat mats as needed.
- Provide bedding materials such as straw or shavings to help piglets stay warm and comfortable.

2. Colostrum:

- Colostrum, the first milk produced by the sow, is crucial for piglet immunity. Piglets should receive colostrum within the first 24 hours of life.
- Ensure that piglets have access to colostrum from their mother or supplemental colostrum if necessary.

3. Nutrition:

- If a piglet does not receive enough colostrum, provide a commercial colostrum replacer to ensure proper nutrition and immunity.
- After colostrum feeding, transition piglets to sow's milk or an appropriate milk replacer.

4. Hydration:

- Ensure that piglets have access to clean, fresh water as they get older and are weaned from the sow's milk.

5. Weaning:

- Piglets are typically weaned at 6-8 weeks of age. Gradually transition them to a starter diet suitable for their age and size.

6. Housing:

- Maintain a clean and dry farrowing area with appropriate bedding materials.
- Monitor temperature and humidity levels to ensure a comfortable environment.

7. Health Care:

- Perform routine health checks on piglets to identify any signs of illness, such as diarrhea. Administer appropriate medications as needed.

8. Socialization:

- Allow piglets to socialize with littermates and other pigs in a safe and clean environment. Social interaction is important for their development.

9. Record Keeping:

- Maintain detailed records of each piglet's birthdate, health status, vaccinations, and any treatments given. This information is valuable for management decisions.

10. Castration and Tail Docking:

- If necessary, perform castration and tail docking on male piglets at the appropriate age to ensure animal welfare and prevent unwanted Behaviours.

11. Proper Space and Housing:

- As piglets grow, provide adequate space and housing to prevent overcrowding, stress, and aggression.

12. Disease Prevention:

- Implement biosecurity measures to prevent the introduction of diseases into the piglet population.
- Keep the farrowing area clean and sanitized.

13. Market Preparation:

- If raising piglets for market, follow growth and feeding protocols to ensure they reach the desired weight and condition for market.

14. Monitoring Growth:

- Regularly weigh piglets to monitor their growth and adjust feeding accordingly.

15. Gradual Changes:

- When making changes to their diet or environment, do so gradually to minimize stress and digestive issues.

16. Veterinary Care:

- Consult with a veterinarian for advice on piglet care, vaccinations, and health management.

By providing attentive care, nutrition, and a clean environment, you can ensure the healthy growth and development of newborn piglets. Proper management practices will contribute to the success and productivity of your swine operation.

CHAPTER 13
HOW TO MANAGE YOUR PIGS DURING AND AFTER WEANING

MANAGING pigs during and after weaning is a critical phase in swine production that requires attention to detail to ensure the piglets' health, growth, and successful transition from sow's milk to solid feed. Here's a step-by-step guide on how to manage your pigs during and after weaning:

During Weaning:

1. **Timing:** Weaning typically occurs at 3-4 weeks of age, although this can vary depending on individual piglet development and farm practices. Ensure that piglets are developmentally ready for weaning.
2. **Gradual Transition:** Transition piglets from sow's milk to solid feed gradually. Start offering creep feed (starter diet) a few days before weaning to familiarize them with the new feed source.
3. **Feeding Schedule:** Initially, feed piglets small meals several times a day to encourage feed consumption. Gradually transition to a standard feeding schedule.
4. **High-Quality Feed:** Provide a high-quality starter diet formulated for piglets. Ensure that it is easily digestible and nutritionally balanced to support growth.
5. **Water Access:** Ensure piglets have access to clean, fresh water at all times. Proper hydration is crucial during the weaning process.
6. **Environment:** Maintain a clean, dry, and draft-free environment for the newly weaned piglets. Adequate bedding and temperature control are essential.
7. **Socialization:** Allow piglets to socialize with littermates and other pigs in a safe and clean environment. Social interaction promotes healthy development.
8. **Monitor Health:** Keep a close eye on piglets for signs of illness, such as diarrhea, coughing, or lethargy. Address health issues promptly.

After Weaning:

1. **Diet Transition:** Continue feeding piglets a starter diet designed for their age and size. Gradually transition to a grower diet as they grow.
2. **Vaccination and Health Care:** Implement a health care program that includes vaccinations, deworming, and routine health checks. Consult with a veterinarian for guidance on specific health protocols.
3. **Record Keeping:** Maintain detailed records of each piglet's health, vaccinations, and growth performance. This information is valuable for management decisions.
4. **Weaning Stress:** Be aware that weaning can be stressful for piglets, which can make them more susceptible to disease. Provide a calm and consistent environment.
5. **Space and Housing:** As piglets grow, ensure they have enough space and appropriate housing to prevent overcrowding, stress, and aggression.
6. **Dietary Transition:** Gradually transition piglets from starter to grower diets as they age and their nutritional requirements change.
7. **Monitoring Growth:** Regularly weigh piglets to monitor their growth and adjust feeding accordingly. Achieve target weights for market pigs.
8. **Socialization:** Continue to allow piglets to socialize with their penmates. Social interaction is important for their mental and physical well-being.
9. **Biosecurity:** Maintain strict biosecurity measures to prevent disease introduction and transmission within the piglet population.
10. **Market Preparation:** If you are raising piglets for market, follow growth and feeding protocols to ensure they reach the desired weight and condition for market.
11. **Consult with Veterinarian:** Regularly consult with a veterinarian to assess the health and welfare of the

weaned piglets and make informed management decisions.

By following these guidelines and providing proper care, nutrition, and a clean environment during and after weaning, you can ensure the healthy growth and development of your piglets. This period is crucial for their overall success and productivity in your swine operation.

MANAGING GROWTH RATE IN PIGS

Managing the growth rate in pigs is crucial for optimizing production efficiency and ensuring that pigs reach their target market weight in a timely manner. Proper growth management involves a combination of nutrition, genetics, housing, and health care. Here are key strategies to manage growth rate in pigs effectively:

1. Balanced Nutrition:

- Provide a well-balanced diet tailored to the specific growth stage of the pigs. Start with a starter diet for piglets and transition to grower and finisher diets as they age.

- Work with a nutritionist to formulate diets that meet the nutritional requirements of your pigs. Pay attention to energy, protein, vitamins, and minerals.

2. Feeding Management:

- Implement a consistent feeding schedule and ensure that pigs have access to feed and clean, fresh water at all times.
- Monitor feed intake and adjust feed rations as needed to promote steady growth. Avoid overfeeding, which can lead to obesity and health problems.

3. Housing and Environment:

- Provide clean and comfortable housing with proper ventilation and temperature control.
- Prevent overcrowding, as it can lead to stress, reduced feed intake, and slower growth. Ensure adequate space for pigs to move and rest.

4. Health Management:

- Maintain a robust health program that includes vaccinations, deworming, and regular health checks. Address any health issues promptly to prevent disease-related growth setbacks.

5. Record Keeping:

- Keep detailed records of pig weights, feed consumption, and growth rates. Use this data to monitor and manage growth performance and to identify potential problems

6. Avoiding Stress:

- Minimize stressors in the pig's environment, as stress can hinder growth. Examples of stressors include overcrowding, abrupt changes in diet, and exposure to extreme temperatures.

8. Proper Handling:

- Handle pigs gently and calmly to reduce stress and minimize injuries. Avoid rough handling that can cause fear or aggression.

9. Market Weight Goals:

Determine the target market weight for your pigs and develop a feeding and management plan to achieve this goal.

10. Biosecurity:

- Implement strict biosecurity measures to prevent the introduction of diseases into your herd, which can negatively impact growth.

11. Consulting with Experts:

- Work with swine veterinarians, and other experts in the field to fine-tune your growth management strategies and address specific challenges.

12. Market Timing:

- Plan the timing of market sales to align with optimal growth rates and market demand.

13. Adaptation:

- Be prepared to adjust your management practices based on the specific needs and conditions of your pigs and your farm.

Effective growth management is essential for maximizing the profitability and sustainability of your swine production operation. By focusing on nutrition, genetics, housing, health care, and proper management practices, you can optimize growth rates and achieve your production goals.

FACTORS AFFECTING GROWTH RATE

Here's a checklist of 12 factors affecting weight and probe variations at slaughter, not ranked by importance as their incidence may vary from farm to farm:

1. Birthweights: A 1g increase at birth can lead to a 2.34g increase at 21-day weaning and potentially a 20 to 30g increase at slaughter. For example, a 100g higher birth weight may translate into a 2kg weight advantage at 106kg. However, the impact on slaughter weights can be minimal.
2. Birth to Slaughter: Up to 50% of runt pigs can reach 7kg at weaning if selectively fed and managed.
3. Weaning: Aim for a 4kg weight difference between the lightest and heaviest pigs in 21-28 day weaning, 4.5kg in matched pens averaging 6kg, and a 5kg difference in pens of 7kg or more. These differences help establish the pecking order more rapidly, allowing submissive pigs to catch up in growth potential.
4. Adequate Trough Space*: Ensuring sufficient trough space is vital, especially post-weaning.

5. Feeder Gap Space*: Check feeder gap space daily. In comparison, checking weekly can widen weight variations at slaughter by 20%.
6. Overstocking*: Overstocking by 15% can also increase variation at slaughter by 20%.
7. Genetics: The predominance of dam lines can influence variability in both growth and grading. Mixing male lines may similarly increase variation.
8. Environment: Extreme temperatures and improper ventilation can affect weight variation.
9. Feed Intake*: Within a pen, feed intake can vary by up to 20%. Providing your nutritionist with estimated daily intakes from each farm (or even each house with a CWF pipeline) every quarter helps adjust the diet to account for seasonality and health changes to some extent.
10. Water Provision: Accessibility to water can be as important as water adequacy.
11. Seasonal Effects: Probe and carcass weights tend to be lower during the summer months.
12. Health: Good health practices reduce weight variability within pens

CHAPTER 14
CARE AND MANAGEMENT OF BOAR

THE CARE and management of a breeding boar are critical for ensuring the success of a swine breeding program. A healthy and well-maintained boar contributes to reproductive efficiency and the production of healthy piglets. Here's a comprehensive guide on how to care for and manage a breeding boar:

1. Housing: Provide a clean and comfortable housing facility for the boar. Ensure it is well-ventilated, dry, and free from drafts. Ensure the housing area is secure to prevent injury and escapes. Boars can become aggressive, especially during breeding.

2. Nutrition: Feed the boar a balanced diet that meets its nutritional needs for maintaining good body condition and fertility. Monitor the boar's body condition regularly and adjust its diet accordingly to prevent obesity or excessive leanness.

3. Health Care: Implement a comprehensive health care program for the boar that includes vaccinations, deworming, and routine health checks by a veterinarian. Keep records of health treatments and observations to monitor the boar's overall well-being.

4. Exercise: Provide opportunities for exercise to maintain the boar's physical condition and prevent obesity.

5. Socialization: Allow the boar to socialize with other animals, including sows and other boars. Social interaction can help reduce stress and improve Behaviour.

6. Reproductive Management: Monitor the boar's reproductive performance and libido. Ensure it is breeding effectively and showing interest in the sows. Record breeding dates, semen quality, and fertility rates.

7. Breeding Soundness Examination (BSE): Conduct regular breeding soundness examinations to assess the boar's reproductive health and performance. BSE includes evaluations of semen quality, genital health, and physical condition.

8. Biosecurity: Implement strict biosecurity measures to prevent the introduction of diseases into your breeding facility. Quarantine new boars before introducing them to the breeding herd.

9. Environment and Comfort: Provide appropriate bedding and clean, dry resting areas for the boar. Ensure the boar's living conditions are comfortable and conducive to rest and relaxation.

11. Monitoring Behaviour: Watch for changes in Behaviour, including aggression, which can be an indication of health or fertility issues. Ensure that the boar's Behaviour is suitable for safe and efficient breeding.

12. Record Keeping: Maintain detailed records of the boar's reproductive history, health, and breeding performance. Use these records to make informed decisions.

13. Replacement and Retirement: Plan for the replacement of the boar as it ages or its breeding performance declines. Ensure a smooth transition to a new boar.

Proper care and management of a breeding boar are essential for maintaining reproductive efficiency and the overall success of a swine breeding program. By providing a suitable environment, nutrition, health care, and reproductive management, you can ensure the well-being of the boar and the production of healthy piglets.

SELECTING WEANERS FOR YOUR FARM

Selecting weaners is a pivotal step in swine farming as it forms the bridge between piglets and mature pigs. Weaners, young pigs recently separated from their mothers and transitioning to solid feed, are a crucial stage in the swine production cycle. Making informed choices in selecting weaners is essential for ensuring the health, growth, and profitability of your swine farming operation. In this section, we will explore the importance of selecting weaners, criteria for their evaluation, and the steps involved in this critical process.

The Importance of Selecting Weaners:

Health and Disease Prevention: Selecting healthy weaners is essential to prevent the introduction of diseases into the herd. Healthy weaners are more likely to thrive and require fewer veterinary interventions.

Growth and Efficiency: Weaners that possess good genetics and have been adequately cared for will grow faster and more efficiently. Their growth potential directly impacts the overall productivity and profitability of the swine operation.

Breeding Stock Potential: Some weaners may eventually become breeding sows or boars. Selecting the right weaners ensures that you have a strong foundation for future breeding stock.

Criteria for Evaluating Weaners:

When selecting weaners for your farm, consider the following criteria:

1. **Health:** Weaners should be active, alert, and free from signs of illness or injury. Check for any discharge from the eyes or nose, coughing, or diarrhoea.
2. **Age and Weight:** Weaners should be of the appropriate age (typically around 21 to 28 days old) and weight for weaning. They should have a minimum weight of around 12 to 15 pounds (5.4 to 6.8 kilograms).
3. **Uniformity:** Aim for uniformity in size and weight among the weaners. This ensures that they will grow at a similar rate, simplifying management and feeding.
4. **Conformation:** Examine the weaners' overall conformation and body structure. They should have a good, solid build with a sleek coat and no obvious deformities.
5. **Behaviour:** Observe the weaners' Behaviour. They should be curious, social, and comfortable in their environment. Shy or aggressive Behaviour can be indicative of stress or health issues.

Steps in Selecting Weaners:

1. **Source from Reputable Suppliers:** Obtain weaners from reputable breeders or suppliers known for high-quality piglets. Conduct background checks, request health records, and visit the source if possible.
2. **Physical Examination:** Physically examine each weaner to assess their overall health, weight, conformation, and uniformity. Look for any signs of illness, deformities, or poor condition.

3. **Age Verification:** Confirm the age of the weaners to ensure they are of appropriate weaning age. This prevents early separation from the sow, which can lead to health and developmental issues.

4. **Interaction and Observation:** Spend time observing the weaners' Behaviour. They should be active, social, and comfortable with human interaction.

5. **Quarantine and Health Testing:** Quarantine new weaners upon arrival to the farm and conduct health testing to ensure they are disease-free. Isolate them from the existing herd during this period.

Selecting weaners for your farm is a critical process that directly impacts the health, growth, and overall success of your swine operation. By adhering to clear goals and criteria, evaluating weaners based on health, age, weight, conformation, and Behaviour, and sourcing animals from reputable suppliers, pig farmers can establish a strong foundation for the future of their swine production. Well-chosen weaners grow into productive pigs, contributing to the sustainability and profitability of the farm.

TRANSPORTING YOUR PIGS TO THE FARM

Transporting pigs to the farm is a crucial aspect of swine production that requires careful planning and execution. Whether you are bringing in piglets, gilts, or boars, the journey from the source to the farm can be stressful for the animals if not managed properly. This section explores the importance of safe and humane pig transportation, the key considerations involved, and best practices to ensure a smooth and stress-free journey for your pigs.

The Significance of Safe Pig Transportation:

1. **Animal Welfare:** Ensuring the well-being and welfare of the pigs during transportation is paramount. Stress, overcrowding, and inadequate ventilation can lead to health issues and reduced production efficiency.
2. **Biosecurity:** Maintaining biosecurity measures during transportation is crucial to prevent the introduction of diseases to your farm. Pigs can carry various pathogens, so minimizing disease risks is essential.
3. **Cost Efficiency:** Efficient and well-planned transportation reduces the risk of injury or stress-related issues, ultimately saving on veterinary costs and improving the overall performance of your herd.

Key Considerations in Pig Transportation:

1. **Preparation:** Properly prepare the transport vehicle or trailer by cleaning and disinfecting it. Ensure that it is well-ventilated, with appropriate temperature controls for the weather conditions.
2. **Loading:** Handle pigs gently and avoid causing stress or injury during loading. Pigs should have sufficient space to stand, lie down, and turn around comfortably.
3. **Grouping:** Group pigs according to size, age, and compatibility to prevent aggression or injury during transit. Avoid mixing unfamiliar pigs whenever possible.
4. **Rest Stops:** If the journey is long, plan for rest stops to provide water and feed to the pigs. Adequate hydration and nutrition are crucial for their well-being.
5. **Handling:** Train personnel in proper pig handling techniques. Rough handling can lead to stress, injuries, or even fatalities during transportation.

6. **Monitoring:** Assign a responsible person to monitor the pigs throughout the journey. Check for signs of distress, illness, or injury, and address any issues promptly.
7. **Unloading:** Upon arrival at the farm, unload the pigs carefully to prevent injuries. Ensure a clean and suitable holding area until they acclimate to their new environment.

Best Practices for Safe and Stress-Free Pig Transportation:

1. **Minimize Travel Time:** Whenever possible, choose suppliers and sources that are relatively close to your farm. Reducing travel time minimizes stress and the risk of injury for the pigs.
2. **Weather Considerations:** Be mindful of weather conditions, especially extreme temperatures. Provide appropriate climate control within the transport vehicle to prevent heat or cold stress.
3. **Ventilation:** Ensure adequate ventilation in the transport vehicle to maintain air quality and reduce the risk of respiratory issues.
4. **Non-Slip Flooring:** Use non-slip flooring to prevent pigs from falling during transportation, especially if the road is bumpy.
5. **Stocking Density:** Avoid overcrowding by following recommended stocking densities based on pig size and age. Overcrowding can lead to stress and injuries.
6. **Documentation:** Keep detailed records of the transportation process, including the source, date, duration, and any issues encountered during the journey.

Transporting pigs to the farm is a critical step in swine production that requires careful planning and attention to detail. By prioritizing the well-being and welfare of the pigs, adhering to biosecurity measures, and implementing best practices, pig farmers can ensure safe and stress-free travel for their animals. Proper pig transportation contributes to the overall health, productivity, and profitability of the swine operation while upholding ethical and humane standards in animal husbandry.

FATTENING YOUR PIG FOR THE MARKET

Fattening pigs for the market, often referred to as the finishing phase, is a critical stage in swine production. Proper management during this period ensures that pigs reach their target market weight with optimal meat quality. Here's a step-by-step guide on how to fatten your pigs for the market:

1. Select the Right Pigs: Choose pigs that are at the appropriate age and weight for finishing. Pigs should have reached the desired market weight range before entering this phase.

2. Housing and Environment: Provide clean and well-ventilated housing with enough space for pigs to move comfortably. Avoid overcrowding to reduce stress and improve growth rates. Ensure proper temperature control, especially during extreme weather conditions, to prevent heat or cold stress.

3. Nutrition: Feed pigs a balanced and nutritionally appropriate diet for finishing. The diet should be formulated to promote efficient growth and meat quality. Consult with a swine nutritionist to develop a feeding program tailored to your pigs' specific needs.

4. Feeding Schedule: Establish a regular feeding schedule and ensure that pigs have access to feed at all times. Monitor feed consumption to ensure it meets the pigs' requirements.

5. Feed Quality: Use high-quality feed and ingredients to maximize growth and meat quality. Ensure that feed is free from contaminants and mould.

6. Monitor Weight Gain: Regularly weigh the pigs to monitor their growth rates. Adjust the feeding program based on actual weight gain to ensure pigs reach the desired market weight.

7. Water Supply: Ensure pigs have access to clean, fresh water at all times. Proper hydration is crucial for growth and overall health.

8. Health Management: Implement a health care program that includes vaccinations, deworming, and routine health checks by a veterinarian.

9. Record Keeping: Maintain detailed records of feed consumption, pig weights, health treatments, and growth performance.

10. Avoid Stress: Minimize stressors in the pig's environment, as stress can negatively impact growth. Examples of stressors include overcrowding, abrupt changes in diet, and exposure to extreme temperatures.

11. Market Timing: Plan the timing of market sales to align with optimal growth rates and market demand. Typically, market weight ranges from 250 to 300 pounds (115 to 135 kilograms) depending on market preferences.

12. Biosecurity: Maintain strict biosecurity measures to prevent the introduction of diseases into your finishing facility. Quarantine new pigs before introducing them to the herd.

13. Observation and Monitoring: Regularly observe the Behaviour and health of the pigs. Watch for signs of illness, stress, or any issues that may affect growth.

14. Preparation for Transport: Ensure that pigs are well-prepared for transport to the market, including proper fasting before transport to reduce stress and minimize waste during transportation.

15. Record Market Data: Keep records of market prices, transportation costs, and other relevant data to assess the profitability of each batch of finished pigs.

By following these steps and providing proper care, nutrition, and a clean environment, you can successfully fatten your pigs for the market, ensuring they reach the desired market weight with optimal meat quality y. Efficient and well-managed finishing is essential for the profitability of your swine production operation.

CHAPTER 15
PIG MARKETING

"IN MOST WEST AFRICAN COUNTRIES, agriculture is the largest industry, employing over 50% of the labour force. Many sectors depend on agriculture for raw materials and as a market for manufactured goods. Food accounts for over 50% of household expenditure in West Africa, in contrast to 12-19% in the United States and Europe.

In the past, buyers and sellers had direct contact, but today's specialization and sophistication have increased the number of participants in the supply chain. This includes distribution, storage, grading, and market information gathering.

To enhance earnings, rural enterprises like pig farming should adopt a market-oriented approach. Adam Smith emphasized that production's purpose is consumption, highlighting the importance of understanding customer needs. Marketing should be an ongoing process, from farm planning to product sale.

Effective marketing is crucial for a farmer's success, preventing the mistake of producing without assessing market demand. In the next section, we will explore pig distribution in West Africa

THE PIG MARKETING CHAIN

The pig marketing chain not only showcases the various stake-holders involved in the journey of pigs from the farm to the consumer but also underscores how this network influences product market prices.

Farmers:

- Small-scale pig farms in sub-Saharan Africa, particularly in Nigeria, often have fewer than 50 pigs.
- These farms are typically decentralized in rural areas, with limited coordination.
- Farmers usually sell their pigs at the village level due to limited access to middlemen and transporters.
- They often act as price takers, struggling to negotiate better prices.

Local Assemblers

- Itinerant local traders visit farms to assess market-ready pigs, typically in quantities of 1 to 10.
- They secure pigs with deposits or commitments and accumulate them for larger truckloads (20 to 50 pigs).
- Local assemblers facilitate connections with middlemen.
- In some cases, pig ownership changes hands multiple times before reaching middlemen.

The middlemen

- Middlemen, mainly from pork-consuming communities in Nigeria, travel to farms guided by local assemblers.
- They negotiate prices, weigh pigs, and cover transportation costs, which can span 400 kilometres.

- Prices include local assemblers' commissions (5% per kilogram).
- Middlemen often rely on transporters for pig transportation.

Wholesalers

- Wholesalers purchase pigs from middlemen at major markets.
- Limited facilities are available for sheltering pigs before sale or slaughter.
- Prices are determined through estimation and negotiation.
- Slaughtered pigs are sold whole or in halves/quarters.

Hotels, Restaurants, Butcheries and Fast Food Outlets

- Some farmers directly supply pork to these businesses, often in bulk quantities.

- Strong relationships with these establishments can lead to stable income streams.
- Pigs are slaughtered, dressed as live animals, and cut into pieces (3 to 10 kg).
- Occasionally, pork is roasted as "suya" or "tsire."
- Modern butcheries are emerging, equipped with advanced slaughtering machinery.
- They purchase high-quality pigs from small and medium-scale producers.
- Butcheries may negotiate payment terms with farmers.

In conclusion, the pig marketing chain in many African countries involves multiple intermediaries and markets, impacting consumer prices. Despite the price disparity, some farmers prefer selling at the farmgate due to prompt payment and reduced transportation risks. Additionally, signing MOUs with hotels, restaurants, and modern retailers offers opportunities for steady pork product supply in growing markets."

The growing tourism industry and expatriate community present opportunities for farmers to establish MOUs with hotels, restaurants, and modern retail sectors. These agreements can facilitate a steady and lucrative supply of pork products to these businesses.

"Identifying Your Target Market for Pig Farm Products

To identify your target market for pig farm products, you should focus on two key activities:

1. **Identifying Specific Buyers:** Define the types of buyers for the specific farm products your operation will produce, such as pork, piglets, or growers. Examples of piglet buyers may include neighbouring farmers, existing farm owners, newcomers to the industry, government agencies, and other organizations. These buyers may purchase

piglets for breeding or fattening purposes, including abattoirs, live pig traders, and processors.

2. **Segmentation Based on Characteristics:** Once you've identified buyer types, segment them into smaller groups based on various characteristics:

3. **Income:** Target customers who have the financial capacity to purchase your products. Consider income disparities and tailor your offerings accordingly. For example, in Nigeria, pork is favoured among low-income individuals, while there's a growing demand for premium pork products among middle and upper-class consumers.

4. **Geographic Location:** Consider the location of your customers and the associated transportation costs. Determine whether your farm is closer to consumers or other markets and weigh the quantities and prices buyers are willing to pay.

5. **Season:** Adjust your product availability to match seasonal trends in pork and piglet demand, especially during festive seasons.

6. **Product Type:** Some customers may buy piglets for breeding, while others may raise them for pork production. Adapt your offerings by, for instance, selling only females at a premium price for breeding purposes.

7. **Behaviour:** Recognize that cultural and religious factors can influence buying Behaviour. Customers may have specific preferences, such as lean meat or fatty carcasses, depending on their market segment.

Pricing Strategy: Your pricing strategy plays a crucial role in your business's success. Consider factors like production costs, competitor prices, and desired profit margins. Be innovative in setting prices, considering options like special prices for new buyers, quantity discounts, and seasonal pricing.

Distribution Plan: Your distribution plan depends on the products you intend to market, whether live pigs or pork. You can sell directly to consumers or work with middlemen who may sell to other traders or consumers. Be aware that the number of intermediaries in the distribution chain can impact your profit margins. Choose your distribution approach strategically."

CHAPTER 16
FINANCIAL MANAGEMENT IN PIG FARMING IN WEST AFRICA

EFFECTIVE FINANCIAL MANAGEMENT is essential for the success and sustainability of pig farming operations in West Africa. In this chapter, we will explore key financial considerations, including budgeting, record-keeping, risk management, and access to financing, to help pig farmers manage their finances efficiently.

BUDGETING AND FINANCIAL PLANNING

Developing a Farm Budget

- Create a detailed farm budget that outlines your revenue, expenses, and expected profit margins.
- Consider all costs, including feed, housing, labor, veterinary care, and marketing expenses.

Cash Flow Management

- Monitor your cash flow regularly to ensure you have adequate funds to cover operational expenses.

- Plan for seasonal variations in income and expenses, especially in pig farming, which can be influenced by breeding and market cycles.

Investment Planning

- Identify areas where capital investments are needed, such as improving housing facilities, purchasing equipment, or expanding the herd.
- Prioritize investments based on expected returns and long-term farm goals.

RECORD-KEEPING

Accurate Financial Records

- Maintain accurate and up-to-date financial records that track income, expenses, and assets.
- Use accounting software or spreadsheet tools to streamline record-keeping.

Record Analysis

- Regularly analyze financial records to assess the farm's financial health and identify areas for improvement.
- Use financial statements like profit and loss statements and balance sheets to gain insights into the farm's performance.

RISK MANAGEMENT

Insurance

- Consider insurance coverage, such as livestock insurance, to protect against unexpected losses due to disease outbreaks or natural disasters.
- Evaluate the cost-benefit of insurance options and consult with insurance providers familiar with the pig farming industry.

Diversification

- Diversify income sources on the farm by exploring additional revenue streams, such as value-added products, agro-tourism, or other complementary enterprises.

Savings and Emergency Funds

- Build a financial cushion by setting aside savings or creating an emergency fund to cover unexpected expenses or income fluctuations.

ACCESS TO FINANCING

Local Financing Options

- Explore financing options available in West Africa, including agricultural loans, grants, or investment programs specifically designed for pig farming.
- Consider microfinance institutions or cooperative societies that offer financial services tailored to small-scale farmers in the region.
- Seek potential investors or partners interested in supporting pig farming ventures in exchange for equity or profit-sharing agreements.
- Investigate government programs and initiatives that provide financial assistance, training, or resources to pig farmers.

Financial Literacy and Training

- Invest in financial literacy and management training for yourself and your farm staff.
- Attend workshops, seminars, and agricultural extension programs to enhance your financial skills.
- Consult with financial advisors, accountants, and agricultural economists to gain expert insights into financial management strategies.

Effective financial management is the backbone of a successful pig farming enterprise in West Africa. By developing sound budgets, maintaining accurate records, managing risks, accessing financing options, and continuously improving financial literacy, pig farmers can navigate the challenges of the industry, optimize profitability, and contribute to the sustainable growth of the sector.

CHAPTER 17
THE ECONOMICS OF PIG PRODUCTION

Expected Expenditure in Year 1

Expenditure	Cost /sow	No of pigs	N	$
Cost of Boars	80,000	2	160,000	320
Cost of Sows	80,000	20	1,600,000	3,200
Sow & Boar Feeding/year*	65,700	22	1,445,400	2,891
No. of piglets produced/year		360	0	-
				-
Medication	500	22	11,000	22
				-
Fuel cost			360,000	720
				-
Cost of feeding piglets*	21,400	382	8,174,800	16,349
Staff and other costs			737,000	1,474
Total Expenditure			12,488,200	24,976

THE OPEX COST of buying and raising 22 breeder pigs, 20 weaners and the piglets produced for year 1 is N12,488,200 ($24,976), including the livestock cost, the feeding, and medication and for raising 360 pigs birthed on the farm and the 20 weaners bought for fattening.

Revenue	Revenue /sow	Naira	US Dollar
Total no. of piglets produced Yr 1	382		-
Mortality (1%)	18		-
No of growers for sale	364		-
Live weight (kg)	80		-
Selling price	800		-
Revenue from piglet born on the farm		23,296,000	46,592
Gross Profit		10,807,303	21,615

The expected revenue from selling the 20 weaners bought at the start of the farm and the 360 pigs birthed on the farm at the market weight of 80kg sold at N800 per kg N 23,296,000 ($46,592. Gross profit N10,807,303 ($ 21,615).

The feeding cost accounts for over 65% of the operational cost. Below is the breakdown of the feeding cost for each weaner. The piglets are brought in at eight weeks (2 months) and fed over five to six months in the fattening pen. A weaner will consume approximately 190kg worth of feed over eight months to produce 80kg.

Month	1	2	3	4	5	6	7	
Feed /day	0	0.4	0.6	0.8	1	1.4	1.8	
Naira/kg	120	120	120	120	120	120	120	
No of days	30	30	30	30	30	30	30	
Cost of feed /mth Naira		1440	2160	2880	3600	5040	6480	21400
Cost of feed /mth $		2.88	4.32	5.76	7.2	10.08	12.96	$43.20

POTENTIAL GROWTH OF A PIG FARM YEAR ON YEAR

NB: Like any other livestock operation, starting with a manageable number is always better and growing your farm organically. This will allow the staff to grow together with the livestock and the farm. The proposed breeding plan for year one is to breed the 20 sows with two boars to produce 360 piglets a year (pig birth twice a year to an average of seven piglets per farrow). Budgeted Cash Flow for the Proposed Production Year below shows the cash flow in the first and second years of the business.

It also shows that the farm can grow year on year to become a large commercial farm without having to buy any more gilts or sows The male piglets will be castrated so that they can grow quickly and achieve a market weight of 80kg within 6 to 7 months.

At the end of year 1, 20 of the female piglets born in Year 1 will be reserved for breeding in year two to double the farm production capacity without having to buy sows from another farm.

The rest of the female pigs will be sold along with the male pigs to the market to generate additional capital. By doubling your farm capacity, the farm can yearly increase her returns year on year without having to buy any more sows from another farm.

Kind of pig proposed for this project

Typically, the best kind of pigs for a farm depends on the overall goal of the farm: For this project we are proposing pig that:

- Is most suitable for your market outlet
- will improve the profit margin of your cost of production.
- has a track record of performance
- will be able to perform better in the farm environment and available local feed

Pristine Integrated Resources Ltd

Budgeted Cash Flow for 20 sows, 2 boars and 20 weaners in Year One

BUDGETED CASHFLOW FOR 20 SOWS- YEAR 1

Month Num.	1	2	3	4	5	6
Months	Jun-22	Jul-22	Aug-22	Sep-22	Oct-22	Nov-22
NUMBER OF PIGS ON THE FARM						
No of Boars	2					
No of breeder Sows	20					
No of pigs birth/mnth				90	90	
No of pigs sold/mnth						20
Cumulative no of pigs	22	22	22	22	22	112
REVENUE FROM SALES OF PIGS						
Revenue						1,120,000
Actual No of pigson ti	22	22	22	22	22	92
OPERATIONAL COST (OPEX)						
Cost of Boar Stock	160,000					
Cost of Sow Stock	1,600,000					
Cost of Weaner Stock	-					
Cost of feeding breede	120,450	120,450	120,450	120,450	120,450	120,450
Cost of feeding piglets						
Cost of feeding weaner	-	-	-	-	-	-
Medication cost	-	0	0	0	0	0
Fuel cost	30,000	30,000	30,000	30,000	30,000	30,000
Staff and other cost	50,000	50,000	50,000	50,000	50,000	50,000
Other cost						
Total OPEX cost	1,960,450	200,450	200,450	200,450	200,450	200,450
PROFIT						
Gross Profit	(1,960,450)	(200,450)	(200,450)	(200,450)	(200,450)	919,550
Profit before Tax	(1,960,450)	(200,450)	(200,450)	(200,450)	(200,450)	919,550
*Provision for Tax	-	-	-	-	-	-
Profit After Tax	(1,960,450)	(200,450)	(200,450)	(200,450)	(200,450)	919,550

7	8	9	10	11	12	YTD	YTD
Dec-22	Jan-23	Feb-23	Mar-23	Apr-23	May-23	₦	$
				90	90		
				90	35		
182	182	85	85	175	265		
				5,040,000	2,082,500	₦8,242,500	$ 16,485.00
182	182	85	85	130	230		$ -
							$ -
							$ -
						₦160,000	$ 320.00
						₦1,600,000	$ 3,200.00
						₦0	$ -
							$ -
120,450	120,450	120,450	120,450	120,450	120,450	₦1,445,400	$ 2,890.80
336,638	336,638	336,638	336,638	673,275	673,275	₦2,693,100	$ 5,386.20
						₦0	$
						₦0	$ -
30,000	30,000	30,000	30,000	30,000	30,000	₦360,000	$ 720.00
50,000	50,000	62,500	62,500	62,500	62,500	₦650,000	$ 1,300.00
							$ -
537,088	537,088	549,588	549,588	886,225	886,225	₦6,908,500	$ 13,817.00
							$ -
(537,088)	(537,088)	(549,588)	(549,588)	4,153,775	1,196,275	₦1,334,000	$ 2,668.00
(537,088)	(537,088)	(549,588)	(549,588)	4,153,775	1,196,275	₦1,334,000	$ 2,668.00
.	.	.	.	.	66,700	₦66,700	$ 133.40
(537,088)	(537,088)	(549,588)	(549,588)	4,153,775	1,129,575	₦1,267,300	$ 2,534.60

REFERENCES

1. https://www.smallstarter.com/get-inspired/how-to-start-pig-farming-in-africa/
2. https://university.upstartfarmers.com/blog/starting-a-modern-farm
3. Economic Efficiency of Pig Production in Oyo State .... http://www.journalrepository.org/media/journals/AJEA_2/2012/May/1337836987-Adetunji-Adeyemo_2011AJEA746.pdf
4. Economic Analysis of Swine Production in Nigeria: A Case https://pdfs.semanticschol-ar.org/1889/0e2a35e4c1cbeaed5cf2e25aebcb538c4507.pdf
5. History of pigs, pork, and bacon | Quatr.us Study Guides. https://quatr.us/food-2/history-pigs-pork-bacon.htm
6. Tried and True Ways to Fail in Farming - Running a Small Farm. http://sportsmansvintagepress.com/read-free/five-acres-independence/tried-true-ways-fail/
7. Why You Should Invest in Pig Farming ? | ITS TRIPPING. https://www.itstripping.in/invest-pig-farming/
8. Pig farming - Smallstarter Africa. https://www.small-starter.com/get-inspired/how-to-start-pig-farming-in-africa/

9. General Information on Pig Trending now - Agriculture Nigeria. https://www.agriculturenigeria.com/farming-production/livestock/pig

10. How You Can Start a Profitable Pig Farming In Nigeria …. https://howng.com/how-you-can-start-a-profitable-pig-farming-in-nigeria/

11. Getting Gilts Ready for the Breeding Herd | Pork Business. https://www.porkbusiness.com/article/getting-gilts-ready-breeding-herd

12. Housing, equipment, and supplies for raising swine. http://waynecounty4hlivestock.weebly.com/uploads/1/9/2/2/19220499/masterstockman-swine.docx

13. Farmers Handbook on Pig Production - SlideShare. https://www.slideshare.net/growelagrovet/farmers-handbook-on-pig-production

14. Basic Pig Husbandry - The Boar | The Pig Site. https://thepigsite.com/articles/basic-pig-husbandry-the-boar

15. Transport of livestock - fao.org. http://www.fao.org/3/X6909E/x6909e08.htm

16. Basic Pig Husbandry - Gilts and Sows | The Pig Site. https://thepigsite.com/articles/basic-pig-husbandry-gilts-and-sows

17. Oestrus or Heat Detection - Pork Information Gateway. http://porkgateway.org/resource/oestrus-or-heat-detection/

18. MANAGING THE SOW FOR OPTIMUM PRODUCTIVITY. https://projects.ncsu.edu/project/swine_extension/healthyhogs/book2000/see.htm

19. Ensuring a successful mating | The Pig Site. https://thepigsite.com/genetics-and-reproduction/insemination/key-points-to-a-successful-mating

20. Breeding Management in Pigs - Management and Nutrition …. https://www.merckvetmanual.com/management-and-nutrition/management-of-reproduction-pigs/breeding-management-in-pigs

21. Managing Sows In Gestation | National Hog Farmer. https://www.nationalhogfarmer.com/mag/farming_managing_sows_gestation

22. Feeding pigs in Africa is expensive. Changing their diets http://theconversation.com/feeding-pigs-in-africa-is-expensive-changing-their-diets-is-the-answer-65171

23. The role of functional fibers in piglet feeds - WATTAgNet. https://www.wattagnet.com/articles/22227-the-role-of-functional-fibers-in-piglet-feeds

24. The importance of water for pigs | Knowledge center .... https://www.impex.nl/en/knowledge-center/the-importance-of-water-for-pigs

25. Nutrition basics | Department of Agriculture and Fisheries .... https://www.daf.qld.gov.au/business-priorities/agriculture/animals/pigs/feed-nutrition/nutrients-diets/basics

26. PROTEIN SOURCES FOR THE ANIMAL FEED INDUSTRY. http://www.fao.org/3/y5019e/y5019e03.htm

27. The role of energy | The Pig Site. https://thepigsite.com/husbandry/feed-and-nutrition/the-role-of-energy

28. Recycled food waste in pig diets can reduce environmental .... https://www.nationalhogfarmer.com/nutrition/recycled-food-waste-pig-diets-can-reduce-environmental-footprint

29. Roots, tubers, plantains and bananas in animal feeding. http://www.fao.org/3/T0554E/T0554E17.htm

30. Feed wastage - carrsconsulting.com. http://carrsconsulting.com/thepig/health-pen/healthmgt/feed/commonprobs.htm

31. Pigs: how to get started – Part 2 | Farmer's Weekly. https://www.farmersweekly.co.za/animals/pigs-2/

32. Good Practices for Biosecurity in the Pig Sector | The Pig .... https://thepigsite.com/articles/good-practices-for-biosecurity-in-the-pig-sector

Printed in Great Britain
by Amazon